Bob,

TAKE FLIGHT WITH DISC!

Merrick Rosenberg

Daniel Silvert

Taking Flight!

Master the Four Behavioral Styles and Transform

Your Career, Your Relationships...Your Life

By Merrick Rosenberg and Daniel Silvert

ISBN: 1453678220
ISBN-13: 9781453678220

Praise for *Taking Flight!*

This is the kind of book that changes corporate culture.
— *Lani Davis, Manager, Human Resources, L-3 Tinsley*

This book should be read by teachers, parents, or anyone who wants to impact others in a meaningful way.
— *Michael Kozak, Superintendent of Franklin Township Schools, New Jersey*

Until now, there has been a void in literature that make the concepts of DISC easily accessible. *Taking Flight!* fills that void. I will be making *Taking Flight!* a part of all my workshops.
— *Bart Puglisi, Vice President, Talent Management, Penske Truck Leasing*

What a wonderfully insightful way to understand relationships. While there is terrific material in here for anyone in the corporate world, I find myself applying its lessons everywhere. *Taking Flight!* is a gem of a book and I will recommend it far and wide.

— Monique Garret, Head of Global Marketing, Octagon Research

Taking Flight! provides a great framework to better understand the relationships that matter in your life. The story is engaging and the model is surprisingly easy to recognize and apply. I found myself using the insights presented here immediately. Your time with *Taking Flight!* will be well spent!
— Maureen ORegan, Director of Technology Strategy, Westcon Group

As an HR professional, I have been using the DISC styles for many years. *Taking Flight!* is a great vehicle for either introducing or re-enforcing this powerful model for understanding human behavior. The fable is fun and illuminates the styles in a clever way. The application section is packed with smart analysis and easy to apply DISC strategies. In a short number of pages Rosenberg and Silvert have delivered both a highly readable and in depth resource.
— Marda Kornhaber, Director of Human Resources, ITT

Finally, an easy-to-read resource that millions of DISC users can reference to improve their relationship management skills. From the parable-like story that defines the major behavioral styles, to the concrete applications of DISC scores, *Taking Flight!* is packed with insights and easy to apply. Managers

will want to keep copies handy for new employees and consultants / trainers will find this a very useful tool for their clients.
—- *Leonard S. Altamura, President/CEO, Steininger Behavioral Care Services*

In *Taking Flight!*, authors Merrick Rosenberg and Dan Silvert have provided an insightful and entertaining allegory for today's often complex business environment. A modern business fable that guides managers to identify, understand and blend individuals' characteristics and compatibilities into an effective team.
— *Gary M. Ilkka, Vice President of Human Resources, Brunswick Bowling & Billiards*

As an educator, I found *Taking Flight!* to be a book that will teach students important principles for everyday life. As a consultant who guides family-owned businesses, I have observed many conflicts that were detrimental to companies and family relationships. I will make this book mandatory for my students and clients. Rosenberg and Silvert do an excellent job of explaining how to understand real-world conflicts and resolutions.
— *Stan Kligman, Clinical Professor of Marketing, Drexel University*

At last! A book about the DISC styles that's both enjoyable and practical. This is the kind of book

that would be very useful in corporate training to get employees to work more effectively.
— *Cathy Sullivan, Human Resources Professional*

Taking Flight! is engaging and provides a wealth of information about applying the DISC styles to build teamwork and improve results. The tips really hit home. This book is the perfect follow-up for those using DISC training initiatives.
— *Chris Kraus, Specialist, Global Talent Management, Campbell Soup Company*

Dedication

Traci, your insight, support, and unconditional love are the wind beneath my wings. Gavin and Ben, thanks for being who you are.

Merrick

This book is dedicated to my wife Cindy, who cheerfully put up with me throughout this project. To Eden, Benjamin, and Jakob, let's take Mom to the beach.

Dan

Acknowledgements

We are very lucky to have had many talented and caring people walk with us on our journey. Our co-workers at Team Builders Plus, most notably, Jeff Backal, Ken Blackwell, Cathryn Plum, Stew Bolno, Aaren Perry, Andy Kraus, Lesley Cruz, Dolores Woodington, Christina Centeno, and Heather Hafner have been enormously supportive in helping this book take flight. To our parents, family, and friends, you have all contributed in ways you will never know.

Special thanks to Traci Rosenberg for her intuitive wisdom and our editors, Cindy Silvert and Melissa Brandzel, whose owl-like clarity humbled these two parrots. We also want to thank Kulin Shah and the graphic artists at 3RDEYE for bringing the characters to life.

Taking Flight!

Master the Four Behavioral Styles
and Transform Your Career, Your
Relationships...Your Life

Contents

Introduction xv

Part I: Taking Flight! — *The Fable* 1
Chapter One: Home 3
Chapter Two: The Forest Grid 7
Chapter Three: The Council 9
Chapter Four: An Old Friend 17
Chapter Five: The Aftermath 25
Chapter Six: If a Tree Falls in the Forest... ... 29
Chapter Seven: Reconnaissance 35
Chapter Eight: The Four Styles 41
Chapter Nine: Reflection 47
Chapter Ten: The Awakening 53
Chapter Eleven: The Home Rule 57
Chapter Twelve: The Stakeout 69
Chapter Thirteen: The Gathering 79
Chapter Fourteen: Onward 83

Part II: The *DISC* Model 87
The History and Mystery of the Four Styles 89
What's Your Style? 89

Style Combinations 95
People Reading 107
Seven Transformative *DISC* Principles........111

Part III: Unleashing the Power of *DISC*.....127
Steps for Reaching Your Highest Potential...129
DISC in the Work Environment.................135
Tapping the Power of Style in Teams..........138
DISC for Teaching and Coaching.................147
Educating with *DISC*...................................149
Better Parenting with *DISC*.........................151
DISC Action Planning 157
Onward...159

Epilogue 161
The Authors 163

Introduction

Sometimes we discover a pattern so obvious and predictable that we can't believe we hadn't noticed it before. Imagine if this pattern could provide a blueprint for better understanding yourself and every person with whom you interact.

Such a framework exists through a simple four-style model of behavior known as DISC. It's hidden in everything we do and it may just be the most powerful tool you ever learn to maximize your potential and influence others.

If you're already one of the millions of people familiar with the *DISC* behavioral styles, the principles shared in *Taking Flight!* will take your understanding to a whole new level. And if you haven't yet been introduced to the four styles, brace for impact: This knowledge will change your life forever!

In our work with hundreds of companies and tens of thousands of people from all walks of life, we have seen how understanding and applying the *DISC* styles releases our highest potential. We have watched mediocre managers evolve into leaders... teams mired in conflict resolve years of pent-up stress...floundering salespeople transform into superstars...frustrated teachers become inspirational educators...and countless careers revitalized and redirected by individuals who have learned how to fully leverage their natural gifts. As they replaced judgment with acceptance, couples have told us that understanding *DISC* saved their marriage, and parents have approached us with joy and relief at better understanding their children.

Whether you're interacting with coworkers or customers, family members or friends, *DISC* can guide you to better relate with others. You will soon understand why you click with some and clank with others. Moreover, you will gain a valuable framework for maximizing your strengths and minimizing your weaknesses.

What you are about to read is not just a story about birds. At its heart, *Taking Flight!* is about *you*. Although you may not notice it at first, before long you will recognize yourself in these pages. *Taking Flight*! is about why you react to your family, friends, and coworkers the way you do. It's also about how you respond to the world around you and what drives your decisions and actions.

Consider what *you* would do in the birds' situation and think about what that says about who *you* are.

Is there anyone in the story who acts like you?

Perhaps one of them reminds you of someone you know.

Do any of the characters push your buttons?

Through behavioral style awareness, you will acquire a new lens from which to view your world. But this knowledge is only useful if you apply it. So with this powerful wisdom as your guide, it's time to spread your wings and *Take Flight!*

Part I

Taking Flight!

The Fable

Chapter 1: Home

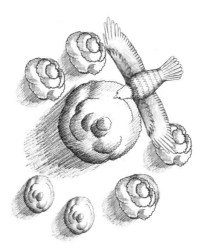

It began with a quiet crackling sound...hardly notice-
able to even the tiniest of creatures. Branches began
to vibrate as the ground trembled below. Soon, the
mighty tree would no longer provide shade for deer
or shelter for birds. It swayed one last time in the
morning sun and then descended as if in slow motion,
shearing everything in its path. With an excruciating
snap, the two-hundred-foot giant hurtled downward,
crashing to earth with a deafening thud.

Would anyone care?

Deep within the forest, known simply as Home, there lived a diverse community of birds. Here fearsome eagles interacted with kind doves. Boisterous parrots mingled with watchful owls. High above it all flew Dorian, a majestic eagle with a proud, sharp gaze. From sunup to sundown, Dorian was on guard. Stretching his impressive seven-foot wingspan, he effortlessly glided on the warm currents over Home. Dorian felt a great sense of responsibility to ensure the security for all those who dwelled below.

With focused attention, he flew over a family of doves sharing quiet conversation. He noticed Samuel and Sarah sitting on a strong, dependable branch preparing a meal for a sick friend. Their soft grey feathers blended seamlessly into their surroundings. Sarah was hatched in this tree, as was her mother, and her mother before her. Cooing in sweet rhythmic tones, they had a calming effect on all those around them.

Dorian sighed and shook his head. He never quite understood why so many birds went to the dove family tree to seek companionship, advice, and comfort—and seemed to stay for hours.

The eagle continued his daily patrol and made certain to watch for Man. The birds enjoyed great harmony in their world, and Dorian intended to keep it that way. If anything happened, he would be the first to know and the first to act.

He soared over the Great Lake and spotted a group of parrots led by fellow Council members Indy and Ivy. Though not large in number, the parrots seemed to be *everywhere*. With a burst of red here and a flash of yellow there, their laughter reverberated from one end of Home to the other. Dorian listened in for a few minutes as the parrots amused themselves with their usual banter.

"We've got a busy day ahead of us. Let's fly!" Indy announced to the clan.

The group happily followed as Ivy asked, "Where are we headed?"

"We'll figure it out when we get there," Indy replied breezily.

They passed just below Dorian chanting their parrot cheer: *"Life's no fun when there's work to be done. But we can make it better if we do it together. Yeah!"*

"Time wasters," thought the eagle as he scanned the forest below. "If they could just channel that parrot energy into something constructive...."

Chapter 2: The Forest Grid

One chilly night as the moon reached its apex, owl leaders Clark and Crystal set out on a mission. After weeks of designing and perfecting their forest map, a source of deep pride to the owl couple, they were certain the map's grid system would enable Dorian to patrol the skies with maximum efficiency.

Clark and Crystal had an innate ability to detect every detail of the world around them. This was coupled with an unrivaled knack for careful planning and organization. On this evening, they diligently employed their skills, working until the sky was orange with the morning sun. As Clark wrapped up his third and final accuracy check, he suddenly froze.

"What's wrong?" asked Crystal.

"This isn't right!"

"What is it?" Crystal inquired. After all, their process had been rigorous, counting trees and meticulously recording their location.

"Well, I guess... we... it seems that... I can't believe I'm saying this, but our tree count is off," stammered Clark.

"How can that be?" said Crystal.

They began to review their methodology when out of the blue—*bammmm, whapppp*! Indy and Ivy touched down right next to the owls and proclaimed in unison, "The parrots have landed!"

Clark rolled his eyes and thought, "Can't they see that we're *working*?"

"Good morning, Clark! Whatcha doin'?" chirped Indy.

The owl reluctantly began to explain the mapping project when Ivy interjected, "Isn't it easier to just fly around and see where the wind takes you?"

Baffled, the Owl's stared back in silence as the parrots flashed bright smiles and took off toward the horizon. Clark and Crystal just shook their heads and returned to the map, trying to identify the source of their mistake.

Chapter 3: The Council

The following morning saw dark clouds hovering just above the treetops. Through the mist Crystal spotted Dorian circling haphazardly over a small section of woods.

In another part of Home, the parrots also noticed.

"Hey, the Big D has found something," said Indy.

Before long, all the birds were looking skyward. Dorian's piercing screech rang throughout the forest, officially summoning the elected bird representatives for an emergency Council meeting. It had been a long time since their last assembly and the entire forest was abuzz with apprehension.

Gatherings were held at the Council Tree, an imposing redwood more than 200 years old. The massive structure featured two wide branches that formed a semicircle just underneath a protruding limb that served as a platform. The Council Tree had also staged many late night, parrot-only comedy sessions called I-Team Improv, a fact that Indy and Ivy chose not to share with Dorian.

The doves, represented by Samuel and Sarah, were the first to arrive and settled into their usual spots. Their calm demeanor hid an underlying uneasiness, as they found it difficult to connect with their fellow birds in such a formal setting.

The doves warmly greeted Dorian, who responded with a quick nod and then acknowledged the owl and parrot representatives. Dorian would lead the proceedings just as generations of eagles had done before him. As usual, he cut to the chase: "We have a crisis on our wings."

A hush fell over the group.

"A tree has fallen not half a mile from this very spot," the eagle declared.

"Hey, we saw that tree a few days ago," Ivy interjected. "It was right near The Road and there were some wolves hanging around. We were wondering—"

"You *saw* the tree a few days ago and didn't report it to me?" Dorian exclaimed as he puffed up his brown chest feathers. "Don't you understand? All of our trees are now at risk!"

Ivy shrugged. "We didn't think it was a big deal."

"Not a big deal?! Do I have to remind you that we *live* in trees? What if this was *your* tree that crashed to the ground?"

Indy raised both wings in the air to indicate that everyone should slow down and relax. "Trees have fallen before and I don't see why—"

"Not like this one," Dorian interrupted. "I'm familiar with this tree and it was gigantic and healthy. Trees like that don't just fall. We need to get to the bottom of this. Now."

"Maybe a big gust of wind knocked it down," proposed Ivy.

"Wind?" screeched Clark, in a rare display of emotion. "Trees of that diameter and height don't just blow over. Do you know the velocity at which such gusts would need to travel in order to do that? My estimate would be...." He began flipping through his journal. "Ah, yes, 86 miles per hour. Enough to knock down many trees, not just that one."

"It was not a natural event that downed that tree," Dorian declared adamantly.

Sarah gasped as a wave of fear swept over her. Silence fell over the group.

"Well?" Indy inquired, nearly bursting with anticipation. "What then?"

"I don't know," Dorian frowned, deep in thought. "But I'll find out."

"First of all," said Crystal, "we all need to stay calm and not jump to any conclusions before we gather the facts." The owl then turned to the parrots. "Let's review the situation. Indy and Ivy, you saw this a few days ago?"

"Yup," the parrots replied in stereo.

"I'm curious," Clark probed. "Why didn't you warn anyone using the Forest Alert System?"

"Didn't think anything of it," answered Ivy.

"Nobody pays attention to that alert system anyway," added Indy.

The doves, who still hadn't spoken a word, glanced nervously at the parrots and then back at the owls, but did not enter the fray.

Clark, having decided that continuing with the parrots would get him nowhere, turned his attention to the eagle. "Dorian, I'm wondering why you weren't flying in the new grid pattern. It's quite efficient and might have allowed you to identify this situation earlier."

"You're kidding, right?" replied Dorian. "Do you really think I spend my days following lines on an imaginary grid?" He snarled. "I don't think so."

Clark began fidgeting with a spot on his wing. "My fellow Council members, we have processes and systems specifically designed to keep our forest orderly."

"Orderly?" Now Ivy, typically easy going, was getting annoyed. "The purpose of Home is not to be orderly—it's to enjoy life. We should appreciate what we have. We shouldn't get worked up so easily. I say, 'Live in the moment, fly with abandon!' Really, I still don't see what the big deal is here."

"That's all well and good for you, since you parrots live in a fantasy world," said Dorian. "But real life is not about playing games—though, if time permits, I see nothing wrong with healthy, competitive sports. Life is about *accomplishments.* We're here in this forest to leave our mark. Do you want to be remembered for how much *fun* you had?"

Indy and Ivy shrugged and thought, "What's wrong with that?"

Meanwhile, the doves continued to sit quietly, alarmed that a full-blown conflict was unfolding. Sarah squirmed uncomfortably.

"I don't know what to do," she whispered to Samuel, wringing her wings. "The Council is coming apart. They're yelling at each other and nobody is really listening."

Samuel nodded and put his wing around her, trying to be soothing even though he was upset, too. "We can't resolve anything by acting like this. We have to work together in harmony or else Home won't be worth saving."

Suddenly, Sarah had an idea.

"I think we need some outside help," she said.

"Xavier?" Samuel asked.

"The birds in the north are still talking about how he changed their lives after the big fire. It's worth a try."

Just then, Crystal turned to Sarah and asked for her opinion.

Sarah was caught off guard. She hadn't planned to speak and didn't want to sound critical, but now all eyes were on her. She took a deep, calming breath to steady her nerves. "Well, I can see everyone's perspective," she began warmly. "I agree with Clark's desire for order. We don't want to live in chaos. And I also see Dorian's point that one should seek to achieve great things. As for what Ivy was saying, I certainly agree that life ought to be enjoyed."

Everyone reluctantly nodded in agreement.

"I guess I just want to live in a place where we can all be friends and feel safe," Sarah concluded.

Suddenly, Dorian thrust a wing forward to stop the conversation. He had tried to listen patiently, but enough was enough.

"What are you all talking about?!" he hollered. "With all due respect to our little philosophical chat, we've got a crisis here and I'm going to figure out what's going on. I suggest that you do the same. Let's all go see what we can find out and reconvene tomorrow at dawn. If anyone observes anything suspicious, report it to me immediately."

The eagle leapt from his perch, and with a few mighty pumps of his wings, he was gone. With that, the meeting ended. The group remained silent for a few moments and then slowly adjourned.

Although the birds had all lived in the same forest for many years—interacting on a daily basis, sharing rites of passage and many good times—they had never faced a challenge like this before. Now, an uneasy mood hung over the forest. The Council meeting had, well, ruffled some feathers.

Chapter 4: An Old Friend

The next day, Samuel and Sarah rose early to journey toward the northern tip of Home. Flying side by side, the doves passed over rolling hills and a towering waterfall. Following a creek that wound its way around mossy rocks, they noticed two humans gathering branches, presumably for a campfire. Gliding silently, Samuel and Sarah circled the red granite boulder where their trusted old friend Xavier could often be found. They almost missed him, as his chameleon skin blended effortlessly into the stone.

After a pleasant catch-up conversation, Samuel broached the subject of their visit. Surprisingly, Xavier already knew about the fallen spruce and had even heard about the Council meeting.

"But how did you find out?" asked Sarah.

"Let's just say a little bird told me," replied Xavier with a twinkle in his eye. "The Council meeting didn't sound particularly harmonious."

"That's an understatement," acknowledged Samuel.

"We don't know what to do," sighed Sarah.

The chameleon grinned slightly. "You once knew what to do, but over time, your kind has forgotten."

Puzzled, Samuel asked, "We knew what to do about falling trees?"

"That's not what I mean," replied Xavier. "Consider this: How do you suppose chameleons have managed to survive and thrive for so long? After all, most who live in this forest are far more powerful. And it's not about intelligence, although we have accumulated and passed down much wisdom over time."

He paused. The doves looked at him blankly as the question lingered.

"The secret, my friends, is adaptability," Xavier answered.

"But we can't change our color like you can," said Sarah.

"True. But real adaptability is not related to appearance. It's much deeper than that. In fact, this knowledge is the key to the challenge before you."

Intrigued, Samuel and Sarah asked Xavier to continue.

"Very well then," he added, "but I must remind you to be careful what you ask for. I cannot tell you what to do. I can only offer what I see."

With that, Xavier looked at them intently and declared, "You birds simply do not know each other."

Both doves cocked their heads. This didn't sound right.

Sarah hesitated, then spoke softly. "I don't mean any disrespect, Xavier, but we've known each other for generations. My mother was best friends with Crystal's mother."

Samuel chimed in, "And my father shared many stories of his experiences with both Dorian's father and grandfather."

"And when we were young," Sarah added, "we often played with Indy, Ivy, and the rest of the parrots. Of course, they were a bit wild for us, but it was never boring. I think we know each other quite well."

The chameleon smiled gently. "Allow me to clarify," he replied. "You have shared many experiences, but you do not truly *understand* each other and this has prevented you from solving this crisis." He took a step toward them.

"Long ago, my chameleon ancestors learned that animals have four distinct styles of behavior. This understanding has been the key to our survival—

and now, I'd like to share it with you. Let's look at your bird community."

Xavier picked up a small stick and drew an "X" on the ground. At the upper-left corner, he wrote the letter "D." At the upper right, he drew an "I." At the bottom right, he added an "S," and at the bottom left, he placed a "C."

The doves looked on as Xavier continued. Where was he going with this?

"Each of you has a distinct style, a certain way of expressing yourself and interpreting your world. If you truly understood how these four different styles behaved, communication and cooperation would be easy. Unfortunately, you and your Council members lack this awareness."

Just then, the chameleon's body transformed into a stately golden brown.

"Wow!" Samuel exclaimed. "You look like Dorian!"

Xavier grinned. "Now think about what Dorian is like on the inside. He possesses dominant leadership skills such as decisiveness, vision, and an eagerness to take charge. He communicates directly and is extremely driven to achieve results."

"That's true," said Sarah. "I just wish he listened better."

"Dorian *is* a good listener, if one understands *how* he does so," Xavier explained. "Dorian does not listen with patience and empathy like you do. His style is to quickly assess the bigger picture and offer solutions. He listens for the bottom line. That's not a poor listener, that's a problem solver."

"Well," said Samuel. "I never thought of it that way."

Just then, the chameleon's skin burst into a rainbow of purples, reds, greens, yellows, and blues. Samuel and Sarah laughed. They knew exactly who he looked like now.

"Just like the colors that brighten their feathers," began Xavier, "the parrots add life to the forest. They display sunny optimism and live in the moment—which, for them, always seems to be filled with fun and excitement. They love interacting with groups and are quite effective at influencing others through their passion and enthusiasm."

"Yep, that's them," confirmed Samuel. "My mother always said that parrots could sell ice to penguins."

"Indeed," responded Xavier. "They also bring fresh ideas and creative solutions where others only see dead ends."

The chameleon's belly suddenly turned snowy white while his body transformed into a rich owl tan.

"Clark and Crystal are in their element with small, often overlooked details. They instinctively analyze the world around them and reveal patterns about how things function and interconnect. Then they create systems to provide structure. Accuracy means *everything* to Clark and Crystal, because without quality data there is no solid basis from which to make sound decisions."

Sarah remarked, "I always thought the owls were just being controlling by trying to tell everyone how to do things."

"They may provide a framework for doing things, but they're trying to be helpful, not controlling," said Xavier.

Just then, the chameleon turned a gentle grey.

"Hey," Sarah laughed. "That's us!"

"You don't need to explain doves," said Samuel with uncharacteristic confidence. "We know ourselves."

"Ah, my friends, self-awareness is far more difficult to achieve than you may realize," Xavier sighed. "As Xanadu, the great chameleon philosopher, once said, 'To know oneself is the highest form of wisdom.'"

He paused briefly out of respect for Xanadu, then resumed.

"You bring harmony and connection to your forest-mates. You care deeply about the happiness of others and listen with empathy and compassion. You are patient and calm, attracting others to confide in you when they are troubled. And while your steady energy is comfortable with gradual change, sudden disruptions that radically alter the status quo are difficult for you to cope with."

"Like fallen trees?" asked Samuel with a laugh.

"Exactly!" confirmed Xavier, returning to his native shade of tan.

"You really *do* know us!" exclaimed Sarah.

"This is a lot to digest," said Samuel. "I'm not even sure what it all means."

"What it means," Xavier replied, "is that there's a lot of room for misunderstanding each other. But with even this basic understanding of the four styles—D, I, S, and C—you can begin to appreciate the strengths and challenges of those who differ from you."

"I'd imagine that if we all understood the four styles, we'd live in greater harmony," acknowledged Samuel.

"And with less conflict," added Sarah.

The doves smiled, suddenly realizing that even their responses were in line with their newly identified style. They spent the rest of the afternoon with their chameleon friend, delving deeper into discussion as night fell on Home.

Chapter 5: The Aftermath

The next day, the entire parrot clan gathered together, feeling uncharacteristically upset over the Council meeting. Ivy felt that Dorian's view of Home was paranoid and Indy didn't appreciate the eagle's dismissive tone. Clearly, things had gotten out of hand.

"We don't live in a 'fantasy world,'" Indy fumed to his fellow parrots. "This *is* reality. We look for the bright side because it's obviously there for anyone to see!"

"If the bright side isn't there," replied Ivy, "then how come we keep finding it?"

"Ya' got that right!" exclaimed Iggy, a senior member of the clan.

"Hey, remember when we got back from vacation last winter? Even the owls said it was less fun without us," recalled Iris, a young parrot in the crowd.

"Yeah," said Iggy. "When we're gone they miss the energy. But when we're here, they complain that we live in a fantasy world!"

All the parrots agreed.

Suddenly, Iris leapt off her branch and headed straight up to the clouds. Iggy, Indy, and Ivy followed right behind. All at once, they stopped flapping and started to drop like rocks, screaming "Swaaaaaaaaaan diiiiiiiiiiiiiiiiiiiive!" The bird that fell closest to the ground without crashing won the game.

They hadn't played Swan Dive for a while—not since the Ira incident—but today, it seemed like the right thing to do.

Their familiar, happy shrieks reverberated throughout Home, delighting some and annoying others. "If one of those crazy parrots hits the ground again," thought Dorian, "I am *not* going to help this time!"

Not far off, Clark and Crystal each reflected privately on the day's events. Eventually, Crystal broke the silence.

"Clark, don't be upset about Dorian and the grid. He means well."

"I'm not upset," Clark stated flatly.

"Really?" asked Crystal. "I would be if I were you."

"Well, I'm not," he reiterated as he dusted off his feathers.

After a few minutes of cleaning the same spot over and over again, Clark erupted.

"You do realize that Dorian would have seen the problem immediately if he had followed our system? The fact that he just flies around up there admiring his 'big picture' without bothering to analyze what's happening down here in the real world is an outrage. And furthermore—"

"So you're not upset?" Crystal interrupted.

"Of course not!" exclaimed Clark. "And don't get me started on those shrieking parrots."

"I understand," affirmed Crystal.

"Of course you do!" continued Clark. "They are completely oblivious to what's going on and they have no sense of responsibility. Don't they understand the value of structure? They are so...*random*! How do they manage to feed themselves and keep their nests? It's inconceivable! The parrots have no respect for what owls contribute to Home. Without us, this forest would be chaos."

"They seem to do just fine to me," smiled Crystal. "I'm just glad you're not upset."

"I wouldn't dream of it," Clark insisted.

Chapter 6: If a Tree Falls in the Forest...

Two days passed and all was not well at Home. A tree had fallen and its impact was echoing throughout the forest. Tension hung in the air like heavy fog. The sweet morning songs were muted and most of the birds remained confined to their trees.

The owls pored over the Council meeting minutes, intensely discussing various hypotheses and options. Meanwhile, the doves gathered in small groups, but didn't discuss the fallen tree, as they didn't want to escalate the situation into a full-blown crisis. That wouldn't serve anyone.

The parrots, by contrast, remained hopeful and upbeat. They tried to deflect the increasing tension with humor, which only put the owls more on edge.

Dorian flew on patrol like a bird on a mission, resentful that nobody else shared his sense of urgency. At the same time, he was happy to be in command. And while he would never admit it, the heightened state of alertness made him feel more alive than ever. His intense focus and determination reassured the doves. Even Clark appreciated Dorian's resolve, though he still wished he had followed the grid.

The eagle had no desire to engage in the drama of the crisis with the others. He chose to rise above it all and view the situation from 10,000 feet.

On Dorian's fourth pass of the forest, something caught his eye. He spotted an open space in a densely populated area where he was certain a tree had always stood. The eagle banked hard to the right, then lowered to an altitude just above the canopy. What he saw next got his adrenaline pumping.

A large, mature elm with broad limbs and a sturdy base lay flat along the north bank of the Great Lake. Dorian's heart beat wildly as swooped closer and spotted a second tree that had also been ripped from its foundation.

Immediately the eagle kicked into gear, sounding the alarm and bolting toward the parrots, who were weaving in and out of a nearby grove of hemlocks.

"Trees down!" he shouted. "Two more trees are down!"

Dorian landed high atop the tallest oak as parrots swooped in from every direction, surrounding the eagle in a rainbow of curiosity.

"Two more have fallen. I cannot overstate the magnitude of this situation," he declared. "We've all seen dead trees collapse and live trees fall from lightning. But trees of this size just don't come down like this. Our number one priority must be to determine why this has happened and figure out how to stop it from happening again."

Delivering bullet-like directives, Dorian instructed the parrots to gather forensic data from the scene of the crime, concluding with a brisk "Any questions?"

Without a word from anyone, the eagle offered a quick nod and soared away. The parrots then flew off in unison to what was now known as Crash Site 2.

Minutes later, the eagle passed over the Great Lake, landing with a thud between Clark and Crystal, startling both owls awake.

"Gather the rest of the owls," Dorian commanded. "I need to speak with them."

Unaccustomed to being roused under a hot sun, the owls slowly lifted their sleepy heads while the eagle impatiently tapped his toe.

Dorian updated the owls and instructed them to fan out and interview as many creatures as possible. "See if anyone heard or saw anything," he instructed. "If they did, report directly back to me immediately."

"What would you like us to ask them?" inquired Crystal.

"Just find out what they know," answered Dorian, as he crouched down for takeoff.

"What if—?" another owl began to ask, but the eagle was already gone.

Taking flight, Dorian did not hear the same flurry of activity that followed his parrot departure. He looked back and was horrified to see the owls gathering in a circle, pulling out pens and paper. Rather than setting out to interview potential witnesses, they were...*writing*.

"What the—?" Dorian made an abrupt U-turn and announced to the startled owls, "This is not the time to take notes! You need to get going *now*. Conduct interviews and report back to me."

Departing again, he thought, "They have no sense of urgency. I don't know how they get anything done."

None of the owls liked how Dorian had spoken to them.

"Who does he think he is?" thought Clark. "What gives him the right to boss us around? He doesn't understand that our systems enable the results that he supposedly cares so much about. As my father always said, 'Aim twice, strike once.'"

With a dismissive look in Dorian's direction, a defiant Clark declared, "Let's do this *right*."

Meanwhile, on the other side of the Great Lake, Indy, Ivy, and some parrot friends arrived at Crash Site 2. As they approached the scene, they spotted a pack of wolves splashing in the water, then fleeing along The Road.

The parrots gazed at the mighty fallen tree.

"These trees are whoppers," marveled Indy. "Look at the size of them!"

"Were there any nests?" asked Ivy.

"One, but it was abandoned a while ago, so no real harm was done," replied Iris happily.

"So what are we looking for anyway?" asked Indy.

"Clues!" shouted Iggy. "We get to be detectives."

"That's awesome," agreed Indy, then cocked his head. "Hey, why are there wood chips everywhere?"

"Well," said Ivy, "this *is* a forest. Wood *should be* everywhere."

"You know," Indy realized, "if we solve this mystery, we'll be the heroes of Home!"

"That's right," nodded Iggy, "and we'll have a parade. Our names will go down in Home *history*."

"Imagine what the owls and eagles will think," added Ivy. "They'll realize there's more to us than just having fun."

"And you know what?" said Iris. "After the parade, we could establish a holiday to celebrate our discovery."

"Totally," agreed Indy.

Suddenly, Iggy spotted something that looked like an old piece of red cloth.

"Check this out, guys," he said. "I think it's called a bandana."

"Well, I think it's called litter," Indy chimed in, giving Ivy a playful nudge.

But Ivy was busy looking at the fallen tree. She pointed to the ground with a quizzical expression. "The branches are missing."

"That's weird," noted Indy, "but hardly worth tracking down Dorian for. Hey guys, it's getting dark. Let's head back and get a fresh start in the morning."

And with that, the parrots took off in a flurry of color.

At dusk, the owls were still busy crafting perfectly worded interview questions.

Chapter 7: Reconnaissance

Two days later, everyone met again at the Council Tree to discuss their findings. Clark fixed his gaze upon the parrot representatives. "Indy and Ivy, what did you find out?"

"Let me tell you," replied Indy excitedly, "we got tons of information."

"Loads of good stuff," added Ivy. "For starters, we saw a pack of wolves at the scene."

"I don't think wolves took down a tree," noted Dorian dismissively. "What else did you find?"

"Well, the branches were gone," said Indy.

"Gone?" asked Crystal.

"Where did they go?" asked Dorian.

"They didn't *go* anywhere," Ivy responded. "They were just gone."

"Were there marks on the stumps where the branches had been?" probed Clark. "Did you inspect the area to ascertain what might have happened to them?"

Ivy looked at Indy. Indy looked at Ivy. An uncomfortable silence settled over the Council.

"Look," Indy said defensively, "it had just rained, so the ground was all muddy. There wasn't really anything to look at other than wood chips scattered around. The branches were just gone."

Clark frowned. "That's it? That's what you call a 'ton of information'? Did you assess the splatter pattern of the chips? Do you have a diagram of the scene for us to review?"

Ivy looked at Indy. Indy looked at Ivy.

Clark shook his head in disbelief.

Dorian scowled, then said, "Okay. Let's move on. Clark, what did you and Crystal find out?"

"Well, unlike the self-proclaimed 'I-Team' of Indy and Ivy, our information was limited to those creatures who were in a position to know what had actually transpired. Crystal and I set out at 6:00 a.m. sharp yesterday for Crash Site 2. We immediately identified seven potential creatures to interrogate: two amphibians—a frog and a lizard; two reptiles— a snake and an alligator; and three mammals—a fox, a chipmunk, and a groundhog. The order in which we approached our potential witnesses required an analysis of their daily routines so that we could—"

"Seven?" whispered Indy to Ivy. "We could have spoken to fifty."

Dorian just stared with his eyes open wide.

"He must be impressed," thought Crystal.

And then, the eagle erupted. "You *cannot* be serious!"

"You don't like the plan?" inquired Clark.

"The plan?" snarled Dorian incredulously. "I don't even like the *idea* of the plan!"

"Obviously," a resolute Clark explained, "you are incapable of comprehending the meticulous care that we have employed to determine the most logical course of action—"

"Okay," Dorian interrupted. "So what did you find out?"

Clark sighed. "I'm getting to that. As I was saying, we created an interview schedule that allowed us to acquire information regarding—"

"*What* did you find out?" repeated a now-thoroughly agitated Dorian.

"Well, the interviews were not as fruitful as we had anticipated," conceded Crystal.

"Did you discover *anything*?!" bellowed Dorian.

"Well, nothing yet, but…"

Dorian raised his wings in defeat as Indy and Ivy smugly looked on.

"Nobody had the capacity to tell us anything of value," continued Clark. "But it should be noted that we now have a process that will allow us to efficiently gather information should there be another occurrence of—"

Indy jumped in. "You must have learned *something.*"

"Well...um...the chipmunk seemed particularly suspicious," noted Clark. "As soon as we began, he immediately fled up the nearest tree!"

"How did you approach him?" inquired Ivy.

"After careful consideration, I opened with, 'Where were you and what were you doing yesterday at precisely 10:15 a.m.?'"

"I guess that's owl for 'How ya' doin'?'" Indy smirked.

"Wow," added Ivy. "I'll bet the other creatures couldn't wait to hang out with you!"

"We weren't there to 'hang out,'" Clark responded calmly. "And at least *I* would know how to assess crime scene evidence that was clearly plain as day. What were you two doing there? Fantasizing about your victory parade?!"

Indy looked at Ivy. Ivy looked at Indy.

Dorian was beside himself. "This is unacceptable. None of you obtained any usable intelligence!"

"Okay, what did *you* learn, Mr. Big Shot Eagle?" snapped Ivy.

In a rare alliance with the parrots, Clark chimed in, "Indeed, O Great One. Tell us what your random 10,000-foot flyovers have revealed. We're all ears!"

Dorian was seething. "Were it not for me," he declared, "none of you would even have a clue about what's happening here! You'd all be just sitting around waiting for the next tree to fall."

"Really," snapped Clark. "Who put you in charge anyway?"

"That's enough," interrupted Samuel in a firm tone.

The other birds turned to him, stunned. The dove didn't speak up often, so when he did, it got everyone's attention.

"Sarah and I invited a friend, and we'd like you to hear what he has to say."

Chapter 8: The Four Styles

The Council representatives looked up in anticipation of a bird coming in for a landing, but just then, a voice that seemed to come from the tree itself startled them all.

"Thank you for having me," it said, as if a branch had come alive.

Sitting beside Sarah was the chameleon, Xavier.

When the Council members realized who had spoken, they stared at him uncomfortably. Clark was the first to speak. "Non-avian creatures are strictly prohibited from Council meetings unless approved of by a two-thirds majority vote."

"We're sorry, Clark," explained Sarah, "but given everyone's sensitivity over the crisis, we felt that we needed some outside support."

"Bold move," thought Dorian, impressed by the doves' initiative. "I hope *he* knows something."

Xavier scurried up to the podium and silently examined the assemblage of birds. Finally, he spoke. "So many colors to choose from," he marveled. "What great diversity in this group. It's too bad you don't appreciate it."

"That's because right now there's not much to appreciate!" mumbled Dorian.

The chameleon crawled down from the podium and beckoned the birds to form a small circle around him. The eagle and owls found it awkward being so close to the others, but grudgingly complied. Samuel and Sarah felt right at home. They loved nesting like this.

Xavier explained the four different styles to the group: the decisiveness of the *D*, the enthusiasm of the *I*, the compassion of the *S*, and the accuracy of the *C*. The chameleon then took a step back and sat quietly.

"So," Clark asked, "what does this mean for us?"

The chameleon slowly turned his gaze from one Council member to the other, transforming into a dazzling collage of colors representing all of the birds. The doves smiled at each other.

"Sure," said Ivy, "that's easy for you to do, you're a chameleon!"

"Actually," replied Xavier, "it's not a simple feat to assume the color of those around you."

This surprised the birds, who knew little about other species.

"For me to display your color, I must understand you," he explained. "When I look at Dorian, I feel his confidence and authority. This understanding allows me to assume his appearance. When I look at the parrots, I experience excitement and freedom. Life is suddenly full of opportunity and optimism. With the owls, I sense precision and order. I experience a structured world that ensures quality and accuracy. And when I connect to the doves, I feel harmony and compassion. I experience a sincere caring for the well-being and happiness of others."

The doves tingled with excitement. For the first time since the initial tree fell, they felt the group was coming together.

Suddenly, Dorian snapped, "Are you saying that I should *hang out* with the parrots just for kicks, and complicate anything and everything to better understand the owls? I can't do that. I'd be neglecting my leadership responsibilities, not to mention wasting my time!"

"Oh *paa-leeeeease*," interjected Indy. "What has all your *leadership* actually amounted to?"

Samuel and Sarah sighed in disappointment.

Clark studied the chameleon carefully. "I must say that while I find the four styles fascinating, I have no intention of abandoning logic and analysis in favor of these other...ahem...*qualities* you have described in the others."

Sarah was upset. She had worked hard to unite the group. It took a lot for her to stand up to the others, but this had gone too far. "Everyone, please," she pleaded. "Don't you see? This is exactly what Xavier is talking about."

Xavier nodded calmly. "You are all so caught up in your own worlds that you think that *your* way of doing things is the *only* way."

"What's wrong with that? My way works for me. And it worked for my father before me and his father before him," said Dorian proudly.

"Same here," chirped the others in unison.

Xavier flicked his tongue and caught a passing fly.

"Well," the chameleon said, "I'm glad you're all in agreement about *something*. But you need to be more accepting and less judgmental if you wish to solve this crisis and live in harmony."

Clark folded his wings across his chest. "This is a lot to absorb."

"I still don't think you all respect what I do for this place," said Dorian.

"I'm not convinced that you appreciate me and the other parrots," said Indy.

Xavier returned to a wooden shade of brown. Samuel caught his friend's eye, and with a sad wave, bid him goodbye. The chameleon slipped away as the birds continued to bicker.

Before the trees had begun falling, Home had been such a peaceful place. And while they knew that they were all distinct from one another, the birds had assumed they shared more similarities than differences. Now they weren't so sure.

It was a cold night at Home.

Chapter 9: Reflection

The birds spent the next day with those of like feathers. The parrots commiserated about the negativity at the Council meeting. There was too much dwelling on the past rather than envisioning a hopeful future.

Clark and Crystal organized an owls-only meeting to review Xavier's theories and discuss their efficacy. What did these *D-I-S-C* letters stand for? Had other owls observed the four styles as well? Was their experience consistent with his model? There was much analysis and debate.

Samuel and Sarah invited a few friends over for a light snack. The group voiced discomfort about the lack of harmony at Home. They now feared that Xavier's insights might have driven everyone further apart instead of bringing them closer together.

As Dorian surveyed Home from above, he flew with a renewed sense of purpose to prevent another tree from falling. While thinking about the previous day's debate, he still felt that his efforts weren't appropriately respected by the others.

Yet, after crisscrossing above Home for a while, Dorian began to wonder if he was judging others as Xavier had described. If so, then as the leader he could very well be a big part of the problem, and that would be unacceptable. Dorian's action-oriented style didn't often lend itself to deep reflection. However, when a mission was at stake, he was quick to find a solution.

Then it hit him.

"What have I been doing?" he said aloud.

As the sun began to set, the eagle made his way to the treetops where the parrots congregated in the early evening. He circled a few times and gathered his thoughts. The parrots looked up, surprised to see the eagle so soon after yesterday's Council meeting blowup.

After touching down, Dorian made awkward attempts at small talk with the parrots, something the eagle had never done before. The parrots didn't know what to make of it, but they welcomed him. Then Dorian cut to the chase: "We need to fix this situation between us so we can solve the real problem at hand."

The parrots all nodded as Ivy responded, "We couldn't agree more. We don't like all the sniping. It's getting us nowhere."

"Agreed," stated Dorian.

He paused for a moment. The eagle was about to eat a slice of humble pie, and he wasn't sure if he could swallow it.

"I realized something earlier today. That little lizard may be right. I haven't acknowledged what you do for all of us at Home. You obviously play an important role."

For once, the parrots were speechless.

Dorian continued. "Remember when that freak windstorm hit a few years back?

"Oh yeah. That was definitely freaky," said Iggy. "It came out of nowhere."

"Yes it did," said Dorian. "That swirling funnel ripped through one end of Home to the other and we barely had time to react. You parrots got creative and immediately found the solution. Having us fly high above the clouds kept us safe until the storm passed. You guys are real out-of-the-nest thinkers."

The parrots proudly puffed up their chests as they relived the episode. They had, after all, risen to the occasion on that one.

"So," concluded Dorian, "I haven't tapped into your talent for fresh ideas. Instead, I've been expecting you to act more like me...and that's crazy. In fact, if everyone were like me, then we'd really have a problem."

With that, they all laughed.

Then Indy volunteered, "I've been thinking about what Xavier said, too—about expectations. I guess I expect others to react to situations like I would."

"I know what you mean," Dorian acknowledged. "I get frustrated when others can't do what I can do."

"Yeah," said Iggy. "I don't get it when others don't enjoy the same things I do."

"And when they don't or can't meet these expectations, we judge them for it," said Indy.

Dorian thought, "There really is more to these parrots than meets the eye."

Then he added, "So it was unrealistic to expect you to respond to things as I would, and vice versa. Truth be told, facing challenges and solving problems energizes me."

"That's because you're good at it," affirmed Ivy.

Dorian grinned. "I guess we all need to get smarter about what each of us brings to the forest. Then we'll be able to solve this crisis. *Any* crisis."

At that moment, the sun disappeared beneath the horizon and the parrots announced in unison, "Happy Hour!"

"Seems like it's *always* 'Happy Hour' for you guys," said Dorian.

"Come on, Big D," said Iggy. "You're coming with us."

Dorian chuckled, suddenly feeling game. "Sure, why not? So what happens during Happy Hour?"

"Oh, you'll find out," Indy cracked.

Chapter 10: The Awakening

The following night, Sarah was startled by a cracking sound. While dozing back to sleep, a loud snap jolted both her and Samuel awake. Their nest slid left, careened right, then began to shake.

"We need to leave *now*!" announced an alarmed Samuel.

"Wake everyone on the east branches! I'll get the west!" cried Sarah.

As the two doves sped from branch to branch, the violent shaking woke a number of doves too groggy to understand what was happening.

"We need to leave!" shouted Sarah.

"What?" responded one of Sarah's cousins, "I can't just pick up and leave."

"Oh yes you can, and you will!" Sarah commanded, startled by the force of her own words.

Suddenly, the tree rocked left and a thick branch crashed onto a nest, trapping two birds and their chicks inside.

"Are you okay?!" Samuel called.

"We can't get out!" they squealed.

Samuel spotted a group of doves escaping from their nests and called out to them. "Over here! You two get on this side. The rest of you, over there!"

Frazzled and shell-shocked at having to escape from their nest only to be called back to the tree, the doves just flew in place—frozen in mid-air.

"*Now!*" commanded Samuel. "Move it! On the count of three, you're going to lift the branch and I'm going to pull them out. One, two..."

Just then, the tree rocked violently to the right and the nest began to slide. The very branch that had trapped the family of birds inside was now the only thing holding the nest in place.

"Can your chicks fly yet?" shouted Samuel.

"No!" the parents responded. "We can't carry them all! What are we going to do?!"

Sarah arrived to see what was going on. The sound of wood splitting and branches snapping grew louder.

"We can carry the nest!" she shouted as she signaled to a group of doves to join her. "You four lift the branch up and you doves get underneath. We're going to catch the nest as it slides down and carry it on our backs to the ground!"

"What?!" a chorus of doves exclaimed in shock. "We can't! We've never done that before!"

"Well, you're going to do it now," declared Samuel, smiling proudly at Sarah.

The tree violently jerked backward. The first group used the momentum to lift up the branch. The nest immediately slid down and the family strained as they firmly held onto their chicks. The tree leaned further away and the nest suddenly leveled out in the air. The family had no idea what was happening. With Samuel and Sarah now joined by many doves underneath, they gently lowered the nest to the ground. A moment later, an enormous crack erupted and the doves' beloved tree slammed into the creek below with a thunderous splash.

The doves huddled together at the base of their fallen tree. Wood chips littered the ground and Samuel noticed a strange set of fresh footprints that led away from the scene.

Sarah sat down to regain her composure. Beyond the stress of losing her home, she had never taken charge in a crisis like this before and needed to catch her breath.

The rest of the doves remained quiet, staring in disbelief.

A short time later, the doves flew off to awaken the parrots and were immediately taken in for the night. Ivy and Indy sat stunned as Samuel and Sarah recounted the night's horrible events.

"*Now* it's personal! We're going to find out who did this," vowed Indy.

Ivy looked at Samuel and Sarah with newfound respect. "You two are heroes!" she proclaimed.

Both doves blushed.

"I will say," conceded Sarah, "I felt a bit like Dorian out there, ordering others around and making things happen."

"Yes," chuckled Samuel, "you did a fine eagle impersonation. I never realized how useful a little decisiveness could be."

Chapter 11: The Home Rule

Within hours, all of Home was buzzing. An emergency Council meeting was called for dawn the next morning. The Council members arrived just before sunup, except for Samuel and Sarah, who were scouting new trees to inhabit.

The parrots were fueled with passion. "Nobody does that to our friends and gets away with it!" declared Indy.

Clark added, "We've got to get it right this time. There is no margin for error."

Dorian stepped up to the podium. He had more bad news for the Council, and there was no time to waste. "Three more trees went down last night at the lake's northern tip. Dozens of nests were destroyed. Fortunately, everyone got out in time."

"Three more?!" Ivy exclaimed, clutching her chest.

"This situation is escalating out of control," Clark stated flatly.

"Look," Dorian declared, "it's up to all of us to solve this crisis. There's no more time for bickering." He stood tall, adding, "I take full responsibility for how our last meeting ended. My words weren't helpful to achieving our objective and I vow to do better this time."

The Council members, floored by the eagle's uncharacteristic humility, nodded in appreciation.

"In fairness, most of us weren't open to what Xavier had to say," Clark chimed in. "And we certainly weren't aware of what each of us contributes to the forest."

Dorian replied, "You're right, Clark. I've been thinking about how we handled the last crash site and I want to try something different this time."

"Go for it," said Indy.

"After the two trees fell the other day, I delegated responsibilities without being aware of our different styles. This time, I'd like each of us to maximize our strengths."

"Excellent," stated Clark, pausing a second before adding, "and if I may say so, right now your decisiveness is what we need in a leader."

"Thank you, Clark. We're going to figure this out," said Dorian. "This time, the parrots should interview potential witnesses to find out what they know. Indy and Ivy will have everyone relaxed and talking to them in no time at all." The parrots beamed.

Turning to Clark and Crystal, Dorian resumed. "You should investigate Crash Site 3. I know you'll gather useful data for us to evaluate."

"Consider it done," Clark said, energized for action.

"Excellent," affirmed Dorian. "Let's meet back here at sunset to review what we've learned."

The birds dispersed and worked diligently throughout the day. The parrots conducted one interview after another as the owls took pages of crash site notes. Promptly at sunset, the birds reassembled at the Council Tree, including the doves, who had already chosen a new home.

Before the meeting began, Samuel and Sarah thanked everyone for their support.

Clark shook his head. "Honestly, you doves always put the needs of others before your own—it's about time we start treating you the way you treat us."

At that moment, what looked like a small twig seemed to be moving slowly toward the group.

Then, it started speaking to the doves: "My condolences about your family tree. If there's anything I can do...."

"Xavier's back!" exclaimed Indy.

"What do you have for us today?" asked Ivy.

Xavier was delighted to see a more receptive audience. "Well," he said carefully, "I can share the principle that has guided chameleons for generations—if you are open to it."

They birds gathered themselves in a semicircle around Xavier.

"You now recognize the four behavioral styles represented by each of your species," he began. "You're on the path to letting go of unrealistic expectations of one another. It even appears you've discovered that we all shine when we play to our strengths. Very good. Your next step is to pay attention to how you *treat* each other. I hold myself accountable to treat others how *they* need to be treated, not how *I* need to be treated."

The birds studied him quizzically.

"I'm a bit confused," volunteered Crystal. "Doesn't this violate the 'Golden Rule': Treat others how *you* want to be treated?"

"Your point is well taken," said Xavier. "In terms of respect, honesty, and integrity, the Golden Rule holds true. But when working with others or simply communicating with them, should you treat them according to *your* needs or *theirs?* Think about it."

The chameleon flashed them a grin, then slithered down the trunk of the Council Tree. Within moments, he was gone.

The birds were not sure what to do next.

Indy broke the silence. "There's big wisdom in that little lizard."

Everyone laughed—until Dorian brought them back to business. "Okay, that was interesting, but I'd like to shift our focus to the matter at hand—the trees."

"If I may," Clark interjected, "I believe that we are observing the four styles playing out right before our eyes. Before we continue, I'd like to understand the process that the parrots used to elicit information during their interviews. In addition, I'd like to share how I obtained data through observation. Rather than *start* with the bottom line of what we all found, I request that we describe our processes first, then *conclude* with the results. Would that be acceptable?"

Dorian took a deep breath, contemplating what Xavier had just taught them. "Okay, I guess I need to treat you the way you want to be treated. So, tough as it is for me to listen to the *whole process,* I will because it's important to you." He paused for a second, then added, "Truth be told, I guess it's important for me, too. To learn about the process, I mean."

Sarah looked at Dorian with compassion. "I know what you mean. Samuel and I just experienced how exhausting it is to work out of our natural style. But I must say, being direct and projecting authority came in very handy last night. I guess we were tapping into our inner *D,* as Xavier called it. Maybe our inner owl, or *C* style, will help us, too."

"Know what?" Indy chirped. "Xavier's really onto something here! I mean, we could all benefit from treating others the way they want to be treated, right? Let's see...we already have the Golden Rule... why don't we call this the 'Home Rule'?"

The Council was in agreement.

"So it is," declared Dorian, glancing at Clark to capture the Home Rule in the meeting minutes.

"Treat others how they need to be treated, not how you need to be treated. Already got it," confirmed Clark, without looking up.

"Parrots, you're up first," said Dorian.

They simultaneously fluttered over to the center limb of the Council Tree. Indy began excitedly, "It's all in the approach. So, when I spoke to Donna the mountain lion, I just cut to the chase." Pointing a colorful wing at the eagle, he added, "Because she's just like you, Dorian!"

Dorian smirked, "Nobody is just like me!"

Ivy added, "The most important thing with Donna is to be direct and confident. Otherwise, she'll have you for lunch."

"Yeah, 'parrot cake with scream cheese frosting,'" Indy quipped.

Ivy and Indy laughed at their own joke.

"Okay, so what was the bottom line?" asked Dorian. "What did she tell you?"

"Not much," said Ivy.

"But at least we know that she doesn't know anything," said Indy.

"And she agreed to keep her ear to the ground and let us know if she hears anything," said Ivy.

"You persuaded a *mountain lion* to do that for you? That's impressive!" Dorian exclaimed. "For what it's worth, treat me like a mountain lion and we'll be fine."

"I thought nobody is just like you," Indy taunted.

"Keep it up, parrot-head. You're beginning to look mighty tasty," Dorian deadpanned.

Indy shrugged and continued, "Next, we ran into Sally, Sol, and their fawns. Such a nice family! Anyway, their style is like Samuel and Sarah's, so we were patient, soft-spoken, and sincere."

"Yeah," Ivy chimed in, "we didn't jump right into business. We enjoyed their company first and even played with their little guys."

"Wait," said Clark. "I don't mean to cast doubt on your methodology, but how could you gather information while playing games?"

"While we were playing games with the deer," replied Indy, "we were building an emotional connection so they would trust us with information."

"That sounds a bit like manipulation," expressed Crystal.

"Not at all," replied Ivy. "We were simply following the Home Rule without even realizing it! We just treated them how *they* like to be treated. And those kids play a mean game of hide-and-seek!"

"I'll tell you something," added Indy. "The deer were very reluctant to talk about the fallen trees. We wanted them to feel comfortable. Otherwise, we wouldn't have learned anything."

"And...?" Dorian pressed.

"Man has not been sighted for over two weeks," Indy said casually.

"Now we're getting somewhere!" proclaimed Dorian. "What else?"

"Well, then we darn near flew into a swarm of worker bees. We didn't know any of them personally, so we had to be extra careful," said Ivy. "Bees are regimented and exacting...so, just like our owl friends, we spoke to them in a *C* style. We stayed factual and organized and made sure to provide them with sufficient background information."

"Yeah," said Indy. "*That* was exhausting."

"Makes sense to me," confirmed Clark. "But how did you know how to do all this? I mean, how did you know they were *C's*?"

"It was easy!" said Ivy. "They were all flying in perfect formation, spoke in a measured tone of voice, and shared only relevant facts and details. So we tried to do the same back to them, and it worked! The Home Rule is really easy if you just pay attention to what others do. Take us parrots. We're animated and upbeat most of the time. So, if you want to connect with us, just schmooze and share a few laughs."

"So that's the trick," thought Clark. "The parrots make quick behavioral observations and then adapt their style to match the individual or the situation. Quite simple, actually."

As the birds carried on, a brisk wind brought on a sudden chill. The birds instinctively moved from the end of the branch to the center of the tree for protection. Dorian noticed dark clouds gathering overhead.

"Anyway, it took a while," continued Indy, "but ultimately, our new bee friend, Cole, said that their hive was in the first tree that went down. It survived the crash, but came apart when their branch got dragged through the creek and out to the Great Lake."

"What?!" Clark exclaimed. "The branches were removed from Tree #1?"

Indy nodded.

The owl, now visibly agitated, began pacing back and forth, then suddenly declared, "We have to go!"

"Where to?" asked Dorian.

"No time to explain," Clark shot back.

"But there's a storm coming," said Ivy.

Clark leapt from the branch and headed toward the open sky, followed immediately by Dorian. The parrots, doves, and Crystal stood wide-eyed, not sure what was happening. After a few seconds, Dorian looked back over his shoulder and commanded, "Let's go! Follow Clark."

As soon as they climbed above the trees, cold rain pelted the birds in a downpour. In mid-flight, Dorian turned to Clark and asked, "What's going on?"

"In preparation for our crash site analysis," shouted Clark, "we organized a comprehensive list of questions in order to reconstruct and compare what happened to each of the fallen trees, not just the most recent one."

A look of annoyance flashed across Dorian's face.

"Don't worry, my bottom-line friend," Clark chuckled. "We didn't spend the whole day doing this."

A crack of lightning suddenly flashed across the sky—a dangerous reminder of why birds shouldn't fly during a storm. The parrots struggled to navigate through sudden wind gusts as the rain came down in sheets. The doves, who were the smallest of the group, barely kept up with the rest.

"C'mon, guys—we can make it through!" Ivy encouraged. "We can do this!"

A deafening thunderclap reverberated in every direction.

Clark resumed, shouting even louder over the storm, "We identified key areas of inquiry such as 'Were the cut patterns on each tree the same?' 'Are we looking for more than one culprit?' 'Why were these particular trees under attack?' Crystal and I thought maybe their location had something to do with it."

"Clark, I am impressed," responded Dorian. "I truly am. But I'm also freezing my feathers off out here and would very much appreciate the bottom line!"

Clark obliged. "Almost immediately, we observed that some branches were removed at Crash Site 2, but not from Samuel and Sarah's tree at Crash Site 3. Based on the parrots' evidence of branch removal from Crash Site 1, I predict that the perpetrator will soon return to the doves' former tree to remove the branches and finish the job."

"And when they do," hollered Indy from behind, "we'll be there to catch him!"

"Excellent work, Clark," said Dorian.

Sarah smiled. Maybe they could work as a team after all.

Chapter 12: The Stakeout

Drenched and shivering, the birds tried their best to conceal their presence at Crash Site 3. Dorian, the largest member of the group, crouched uncomfortably behind the biggest branch he could find.

"I have to say, Clark," said Dorian, "your meticulous nature has served us well. All those questions identified details and patterns I would have missed."

"Me too," said Indy. "You know, I always thought you asked so many questions because you didn't trust us. Seems that you've just been trying to get the most accurate information."

"Well, of course!" responded Crystal. "We don't mean to offend. It's just about getting it right. Exactly right, every time."

"Exactly right? Every time?" laughed Dorian. "Life doesn't work that way for me. I'll take 'good enough' and move on to the next challenge."

Dorian shifted again, trying to get comfortable. Samuel watched him. The events of the past few days had brought out a bolder side of the dove, and there was something he wanted to say to the eagle.

"Actually, I've often interpreted your...abruptness as being disinterested in our opinions and feelings. But after tapping into some eagle energy last night, I see that you simply want to solve problems as they arise so you can move on to the next one. It's not that you don't care—it's just that you're resolving the situation, not getting caught up in emotions."

"That's just my nature," acknowledged Dorian. "Well, if you were able to utilize 'eagle energy,' as you called it, I guess I can learn to access some dove or owl energy when I need it."

Ivy laughed. "I tell ya', I bet we'll be flexing to each other's styles all the time now!"

"I don't know about *all the time*," said Crystal. "But it's clear that by simply observing others, we can identify their style and understand what makes them tick. And by understanding their intentions, we're less likely to judge them."

"Well said," agreed Clark, noting Crystal's observation.

The birds remained at Crash Site 3 throughout the night, with the owls taking the evening shift. A light rain continued to fall, but the owls remained vigilant.

In the morning, the sky cleared and the air was illuminated by shafts of misty sunlight. Other residents began emerging from their protective cover. The owls jealously watched a few robins unearth some worms. Dorian spied a pack of wolves giving chase to a rabbit. Indy and Ivy were mesmerized by two squirrels spiraling up and down an adjacent tree.

"Hey, Isaac and Irene!" shouted Indy.

"Shhhhhhh!" whispered Clark. "You're going to give away our location."

The birds quietly watched the sunrise as the morning chill gave way to a humid afternoon, and still, nothing materialized. The parrots could barely control their bottled-up energy, but were the picture of tranquility compared to Dorian, who was stewing in a cauldron of resentment toward their unidentified perpetrator.

As the sky filled with reds and yellows, Dorian grew more and more impatient. "This is intolerable," he thought.

Then suddenly, it appeared.

Indy was the first to see it and elbowed Clark. "Hey, what's that?" he asked.

"I don't believe it," said Ivy.

"Of course!" said Clark. "Now it all makes sense! The branches. The wood chips. The proximity to the creek. It's a..."

"I'll be darned," interrupted Ivy.

"It's a beaver!" gasped Indy, loud enough to give away their location.

"We've never had beavers at Home before," added Ivy. "Well, at least that explains why the wolves were there."

Everyone gave Indy a puzzled look.

"What?" he proclaimed. "They say that beavers taste like chicken."

The beaver looked up, and then continued gnawing branches off the former dove quarters.

Dorian's eyes narrowed. "I'll take care of this!"

Samuel and Sarah simultaneously yelled, "Wait!"

Clark shouted, "Stop! Let's talk about it first... *uh-oh.*"

It was too late. Dorian shot out from behind the tree as the rest of the birds watched helplessly. After a few moments, their tension was replaced with curiosity as they observed the spectacle unfolding from a safe distance.

Dorian was bearing down on the beaver, speaking forcefully.

"Look at that!" said Clark. "Nobody communicates with authority like Dorian. He's surely getting his message across."

The beaver dropped the branch he was munching on, transfixed by Dorian's piercing gaze, saying nothing. In response, the eagle grew even angrier, widely gesticulating and pointing at the downed tree.

"This does not look good," Indy cringed.

Dorian, his beak turning red with rage, jumped up and down, shouting threats at the beaver, who just continued chewing.

"Excuse me," asked Samuel, "but is Dorian hitting him with his wings?"

"Nah. He's just pointing at the downed tree," said Indy. "But on a persuasion scale of one to ten, with ten being 'he convinced the beaver to stop cutting down our trees' and one being 'he's just making him mad,' I'd give Dorian…"

"A zero," interjected Ivy.

Dorian stood wide-eyed as the beaver tossed an indifferent glance over his shoulder before calmly swimming away.

"Why is Dorian continuing to shout while our prime suspect gets away?" asked Clark.

"The Dorianator is coming back," Indy announced.

Landing in a furious swoop next to his friends, Dorian unleashed. "He ignored me!"

The eagle stomped around for a while, then finally yelled, "I gave that tree chopper a piece of my mind and he just swam away. Did you see that? He just swam away!"

"Dorian," said Clark, "chopping down trees is what beavers do."

"What, are you on *his* team now?!" Dorian fumed. "That's exactly what *he* said. 'I'm a *beaver*. We cut down trees. That's what beavers *do*.' Well, I'll find him and take care of this."

"Whoa!" Indy's wing shot out, grabbing Dorian's shoulder. "Hold on a minute there, Big D. We need to regroup."

"We need a plan," said Clark.

"Let's all take a deep breath," said Sarah.

Dorian began to calm down and think this through. "Fine. I guess I didn't handle that as well as I could have," he conceded. "But what do you expect? I'm an eagle. I see something that needs to be done and I do it. I don't spot a rabbit and *think* about it. I dive. I attack. I eat. That's what *eagles* do."

"Indeed," said a voice from under a nearby rock. "You were very assertive, but the question is: Was it the right style at the right time?"

Everyone turned to see what appeared to be a sliver of grey limestone gliding toward them.

"Xavier!" exclaimed Ivy. "Boy, am I glad to see you!"

Xavier smiled. "I heard about your stakeout and thought I'd see how things were going."

"Swell," Dorian snorted. "A beaver who thinks he's boss! Imagine! Now we know who's behind this."

"Yes," the chameleon replied, "but how are you going to resolve the situation? After all, the beaver was just doing what—"

"I know, I know," Dorian muttered, "doing what beavers do."

Xavier looked sharply at the eagle, his voice firm. "Dorian, you have great strengths, but *overusing* your strengths won't deliver the results you seek."

The eagle raised an eyebrow.

"You're a *D* style," Xavier explained. "You communicate forcefully, achieving great clarity and purpose. Recall when the first tree crashed, you rallied the other birds and warned that another tree could fall soon. And you were right. Your directness spurred everyone into action."

Dorian nodded, his breathing slowing to its normal pace.

"That said," the lizard frowned, "you sometimes overuse your strengths. And when you do, those strengths become liabilities."

Dorian looked confused.

Xavier continued, "For example, your assertiveness becomes aggressiveness. Healthy confidence becomes arrogance. Taking the initiative morphs into steamrolling others before the best solution has even been identified. Ultimately, this weakens your ability to achieve your goals."

Dorian considered this for a moment and grudgingly nodded in agreement.

Xavier smiled. "But rest assured, my eagle friend, you're not alone."

The lizard walked over to the owls.

"Uh-oh," Crystal grimaced. "Looks like we're next."

"As C's, your zest for asking questions, organizing details, and analyzing patterns allows you to structure your world, as in the case of your tree grid. However, when overused, the C style can lead to 'analysis paralysis,' like when you wasted an entire day creating a massive list of interview questions."

Embarrassed, Clark and Crystal bowed their heads slightly.

"However, more recently, your crash site analysis brought out the best in you. Applied appropriately, your skills led to the culprit."

"Funny how others can see our faults so clearly!" said Indy. "Okay Xavier, now that you're all warmed up, the parrots have braced for impact. Go for it!"

Xavier obliged. "Indy, the I's gift for eternal optimism creates a lively atmosphere and fosters creativity. However, your natural cheerfulness can blind you to situations that are, in fact, quite dangerous. You were the first to discover Crash Site 1, yet you failed to recognize its significance or even report it."

"True," Ivy responded. "I guess that's because we don't see threats, we see opportunities."

"And it's that future-focused optimism that was reassuring as more trees started to come down. You believed that everything would be okay, and your encouragement helped to prevent widespread panic. That was helpful—very helpful."

Turning to the doves, Xavier began to speak, but was uncharacteristically interrupted by Sarah. "Let me guess," she smiled. "Our discomfort with conflict gets in the way of being honest and sharing our thoughts and ideas."

"Exactly!" interrupted Dorian. "During our Council meetings I kept feeling like you had something to add, only you and Samuel didn't say much. But when you brought Xavier to help us out, it changed the way we interact. That was daring, and it worked."

Ivy chimed in. "I guess in 'overuse mode,' your S style was too passive. But when you acted on your need for harmony, it helped us all."

Xavier was proud of his students. "You don't need to change your style in order to be more effective," he added. "You just need to be careful about overusing your strengths, and be able to tap into other styles when needed."

A soft breeze began rustling the leaves of a nearby tree. The group stood for a moment in silence, feeling the warmth of the morning sun. Dawn had ended and a new day had begun.

"So, what are you going to do now?" asked the chameleon.

Xavier flashed one of his famous grins, returned to a grey limestone color, and slithered away.

Chapter 13: The Gathering

One week later, the Council Tree hosted the largest assembly meeting in Home history. In attendance were more than three hundred birds representing Home's avian populations. The air was buzzing with speculation about what would happen next. One especially controversial rumor had the entire bird population moving to another forest to escape the specter of falling trees. Everyone was flapping about it.

Dorian stood up and spread his wings wide. The crowd grew silent. "As you all know, recent events have brought much concern to the inhabitants of Home. Therefore, I am extremely pleased to announce that we have reached an accord with the beavers. Your trees and nests are safe once again."

The audience erupted in wild applause as loose feathers filled the air, blanketing everything in a festive array of colors.

"I would like to recognize key contributions that have led to this historic resolution," continued Dorian. "Please join me in welcoming our marvelous dove representatives, Samuel and Sarah, to the podium."

As the crowd cheered, the two doves reluctantly joined their eagle friend.

"These two don't like to be in the spotlight, but we're going to celebrate them anyway! It was Samuel and Sarah who reached out to the beavers and won their trust. They identified the beavers' fear of the wolves, and got the beavers to agree to stop chopping down the trees we live in if we could get the wolves off their backs."

The birds hooted and hollered, then Indy shouted out, "Dorian, tell 'em what you did next!"

"Well," Dorian chuckled, grinning mischievously, "let's just say that I spoke to the wolves as *they* like to be spoken to...and they won't be bothering the beavers anymore."

The audience roared with delight.

"There's more," the eagle continued as he waved his owl friends to the podium. "In order to coordinate with the beavers about which trees are safe to chop down and which ones to preserve, we needed an ingenious, foolproof plan. Nobody was better suited to design such a strategy than Clark and Crystal. Their Home System identifies trees that are not inhabited by our population. If you plan on moving to a new tree, simply check with Clark and Crystal to verify that it's safe.

"Most impressively, we will now be identifying dying trees that aren't well suited for us anyway. Having the beavers chop down the dying trees actually strengthens the surrounding trees that we like to nest in.

"The owls really thought this through, and let me tell you—I'm glad they're on the Home team!"

The owl audience members hooted happily as Clark and Crystal smiled at each other.

"And last, but definitely not least, Indy, Ivy, Iggy, and Iris, come on down!"

The parrot section immediately broke out in their favorite song, chanting, *"Life's no fun when there's work to be done. But we can make it better if we do it together. Yeah!"*

The four parrots simultaneously leapt from the upper branches and performed a perfectly synchronized Swan Dive, landing right next to Dorian. The entire audience joined in the parrot cheer, wings flapping wildly.

"Okay, okay—" Dorian began. But he quickly realized there was no stopping the parrots, so he just shrugged and sang along.

Eventually, the audience quieted down and Dorian took the floor again.

"Our parrot friends will play a major role in executing our agreement with the beavers. They will travel from nest to nest updating us about which trees are marked for beaver takedown. And, along with the doves, the parrots will continue to communicate with the beavers should any issues arise."

Indy, Ivy, Iggy, and Iris bowed in every direction as Dorian shuffled them off the podium.

Dorian gazed at the sea of fellow birds and a smile spread across his face. "Home is the best forest in all the land!" he proclaimed.

It was clear from the eruption of cheers that everyone agreed.

Chapter 14: Onward

Following the assembly, our heroes found themselves lingering at the Council Tree.

Samuel began, "I think we should make Xavier an honorary member of the Council."

Everyone nodded in agreement, then Crystal added, "That's only been done once before, and it was long ago."

"Right," Clark affirmed, "with Xanadu, the chameleon philosopher." With a thoughtful look, he continued, "Do you think Xanadu shared the same wisdom about the four styles as Xavier did, and it just got lost over time?"

"It wasn't lost. It's obviously in our names," Sarah declared.

"I've always thought that each of our species selected names based on a specific letter because of tradition," Crystal said. "Now it's clear that the styles have been embedded in our culture all along and we didn't even know it!"

"What about Xavier?" Indy wondered.

"He must be the *X-factor*," Clark theorized. "His flexibility allows him to adapt to any situation he encounters."

"This is important," Dorian added. "We should take steps to ensure this knowledge gets passed down to future generations."

They all agreed, and worked together to recap what they had learned as Clark wrote down the ideas on a parchment scroll.

The Wisdom of the Four Styles

There are four distinct behavioral styles: D, I, S, and C. D's are dominant, direct, and decisive. I's are interactive, inspirational, and intuitive. S represents those who are supportive, sensitive, and steady. C stands for conscientious, correct, and consistent.

Understand your own style.

Recognize the styles of others.

Think about style when establishing expectations.

Consider intention, not just behavior.

Use your strengths, but don't overuse them.

Apply the right style at the right time.

Treat others how they need to be treated, not how you need to be treated (the Home Rule).

The sun had just crossed the horizon. Crystal gazed into the distance.

"I wonder if the styles hold true outside of Home," she mused.

"Outside?" asked Indy.

"I'm thinking about one species in particular," said Crystal.

Clark nodded. "Man. Their names don't fit into any known system or pattern."

"But wouldn't it be easier for Man to figure out each other's styles if they used a code like ours?" asked Ivy.

Sarah answered, "They're a lot more complex than we are. Some act like eagles and others like parrots. Some behave like owls and others are like doves."

"Yeah," said Indy, "but here's the crazy part. I've watched them from above, and I can tell you, many are a combination of two of us—like parreagles or dovowls!"

"How confusing," said Dorian. "How do they get anything done?"

"Beats me," said Indy. "We may be complicated, but we're not *that* complicated!"

"Now, if there is no further business, I, for one, am looking forward to the doves' Tree-Warming Party," said Crystal.

"I can't wait," said Ivy. "We've got a few surprises for you."

"Does this mean we're going to find out what happens at your famous Happy Hours?" asked Sarah.

"You got it!" smiled Indy. "But as Xavier once said, 'Be careful what you ask for....'"

They laughed and, taking flight, headed off into the sunset.

THE END

Part II

The *DISC* Model

A model is a tool for the mind.
—*Francis Bacon*

Through Xavier's guidance, our bird friends discovered the transformative power of *DISC*. We hope you enjoyed learning about the styles through their story, and now it's time to consider how it impacts *your* world.

What's Your Style?

While you may have a good sense of which *DISC* style or styles characterize your behavior, the following quick assessment will help you better understand the intensity of each style in your overall behavioral pattern.

Think of yourself in a specific setting, such as work or home. Then, go across each row and assign 4 points to the word that is *most like you*, 3 points to the word that is *like you*, 2 points to the word that is *somewhat like you*, and 1 point to the word that is *least like you*.

___ Assertive	___ Enthusiastic	___ Methodical	___ Questioning
___ Direct	___ Sociable	___ Harmonious	___ Thorough
___ Bottom-line	___ Funny	___ Agreeable	___ Well-disciplined
___ Pioneering	___ Persuasive	___ Patient	___ Logical
___ Authoritative	___ Talkative	___ Helpful	___ Objective
___ Results-oriented	___ Impulsive	___ Easygoing	___ Controlled
___ Impatient	___ Motivating	___ Sympathetic	___ Cautious
___ Competitive	___ Optimistic	___ Accommodating	___ Analytical
___ Decisive	___ High-spirited	___ Consistent	___ Prepared
___ Bold	___ Imaginative	___ Considerate	___ Accurate
___ TOTAL	___ TOTAL	___ TOTAL	___ TOTAL

Now, add up each column to get the total. The first column represents the D style. The second column is the I. The third is the S. And the fourth is the C. As you consider your results, you'll notice that some scores are higher than others. The highest score indicates your primary style. If you have a second style that totals more than 27, you have a secondary style that also plays a significant role in driving your behavior.

The higher the score, the more often you're likely to demonstrate the core traits of that style. For example, a strong D doesn't need to learn how to be direct any more than a high S needs to learn how to be empathetic. It's just what they do.

Environments that are aligned with our predominant style are energizing. Settings that are incongruent with our natural style can be exhausting. Depending on what type of environment we create for others, we either boost or drain their energy.

Remember, there is no "best" style. Every style has its strengths and challenges. Further, style is not a predictor of success or happiness. People of every style have healthy relationships and live fulfilling lives.

<u>Below are the basic traits of each style</u>:

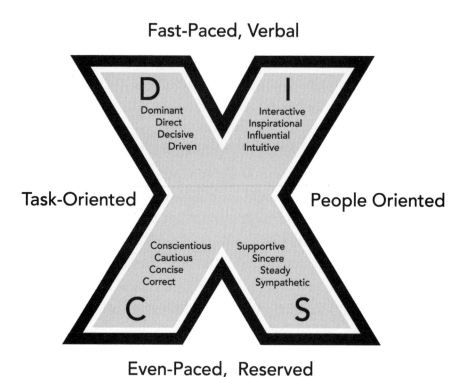

*The **D**ominant style*

Like the eagle, Dorian, *D's* focus on achieving results. They favor action over planning and are typically guided by a long-term, big-picture vision of what can be accomplished. *D's* seek challenges and take risks that will yield big rewards. They can quickly size up a situation and decisively determine a course of action.

D's are assertive, direct, and competitive. They don't like to waste time and their bottom-line nature drives how they communicate. They want straight answers and "call it like it is."

D's are self-starters who challenge the status quo. They thrive in positions of power and seek to control their own destinies. Their tenacity and natural confidence enable them to accomplish even the most demanding objectives.

*The **I**nteractive style*

Like the parrots, Indy and Ivy, *I's* have active minds, seek constant stimulation, and enjoy interacting with people and the world around them. This allows them to thrive in social environments and drives their thirst for adventure.

With their boundless optimism and innate people skills, *I's* are highly persuasive and inspirational. They have fun wherever they go and infuse play and positive energy into all aspects of their lives.

The *I's* intuition and free-spirited nature enable them to create "out of the box" ideas. They don't get bogged down in minutiae, as details would only restrict their imagination. *I's* are future-focused and live in the realm of possibility, where everything is exciting and achievable.

The Supportive style

Just as doves Samuel and Sarah sought to restore harmony to Home, *S's* seek to minimize conflict and create calm, safe environments. *S's* are friendly, compassionate people who patiently listen with empathy. They build deep, loyal relationships and are steadfast friends and partners.

S's favor practical, tried-and-true procedures that ensure stability. They like familiar, predictable patterns that produce consistent and reliable outcomes. They often work behind the scenes and prefer to support, rather than to lead.

The Conscientious style

As with owls Clark and Crystal, *C's* focus on achieving complete and total accuracy in everything they do. They constantly question processes and ideas to ensure that things are done properly. *C's* are systematic, practical, and efficient.

Rather than being guided by the emotion of a situation, *C's* make decisions based upon logical analysis of observable, quantifiable information. While *C*'s often prefer to work independently, their even-tempered nature enables them to remain objective and diplomatic when dealing with others.

Style Combinations

As our friends realized at the fable's end, people can be a bit more complicated than birds when it comes to how they view and interact with the world. In fact, you may have easily recognized yourself in two or more of the characters. Perhaps you are a combination of Dorian and Indy, a *DI,* or of Clark and Sarah, a *CS.* Our bird friends did not exhibit strong secondary styles, but most people do. A strong *D,* for example, reacts very differently to stress than a *DC.* Therefore, the secondary styles can play a decisive role in how we interpret and react to the people and situations around us.

Using your assessment score from the survey you just completed, discover how the styles combine to form your overall behavioral pattern:

DI – The Persuader

DI's combine the decisiveness of the *Dominant* style with the fun, social orientation of the *Interactive* style. *DI*'s demonstrate a strong desire to achieve results, but they do so by embracing collaboration with others. They are highly influential as they combine direct and clear communication with high energy and enthusiasm.

In the workplace, *DI's* are visionary and drive organizational change. They take the lead and embrace risk-taking. *DI's* become frustrated in settings in which they must be passive followers of what is happening around them. *DI's* want to be engaged in creating the vision and executing big ideas, and often gravitate toward leadership roles. They thrive in settings where big ideas are embraced and don't get bogged down in over-analysis.

DI's tend to have a "ready-fire-aim" mentality and benefit a great deal from people who add structure to their world. Moreover, partnering with more detail-oriented people, such as *C's,* enables *DI's* to focus on their core strengths.

In overuse, *DI's* tend to lack patience, which can lead to impulsive decision making. Under stress, *DI's* become restless and externalize their stress, which can create anxiety in others.

<u>ID – The Motivator</u>

As one might imagine, *ID's* are similar in orientation to *DI's*. The difference is that when *I* is stronger than *D,* the individual is first and foremost a motivator. The *ID's* optimistic spirit drives people to action through boundless enthusiasm. They enjoy and even crave constant stimulation. *ID's* thrive in unstructured, free-flowing settings that encourage innovative approaches to achieve results.

ID's build morale in their work environment and generate excitement for goals and ideas. They intuitively sense people's moods and are effective at influencing others to get what they want. *ID's* enjoy forming strategic alliances that advance their ideas. However, their big-picture focus needs to be supported by others who are detail-oriented and think things through. *ID's* abhor negativity and skepticism. They have difficulty working with people so rigid or buried in the details of a project that they fear taking risks and thus miss the bigger picture.

In overuse, *ID's* externalize their stress, which can add frenzied energy to the environment. They can overuse their optimism, which can lead to unrealistic assessments of ideas and people. However, in a crisis, *ID's* are adept at mobilizing the troops for action.

IS – The Connector

IS's are warm, sociable, and friendly. Their compassion for others enables them to quickly and easily build strong, lasting relationships. They are eager to lend a helping hand and are natural teachers and counselors. *IS's* display an interesting mix of self-confidence and modesty.

IS's are the voice of the people. They are empathetic and will not hesitate to advocate for those in need. *IS's* like to work in social environments in which they develop true friendships with their coworkers. They thrive in settings where people care about each other and enjoy personal connections beyond the work at hand.

IS's are less comfortable making difficult decisions that will negatively impact others. They also dislike working with aggressive people who do not respect the feelings of others.

IS's would be well served to surround themselves with quality-focused people who provide structured processes. In addition, they may require others to take charge in high-pressure situations.

Under stress, *IS's* can become overly accommodating and neglect their own needs. With a natural tendency to assume the best in people, they can misread the intentions of others and be overly trusting. Their dislike of conflict can cause them to paper over issues that only grow worse over time, leaving them feeling hurt or betrayed when relationships turn sour.

SI – The Collaborator
Like their close *IS* cousins, *SI's* are easygoing and relaxed, and they go with the flow. The key distinction, however, is that *SI's* focus on *others first,* then themselves. The *Supportive* style's empathic nature combined with the *Interactive* style's enthusiasm culminates in a *Collaborator* "champion of the people" combination.

SI's strive to maintain harmony in relationships. They love to work in team settings and are committed to treating people with respect. *SI's* can be counted on to patiently lend an ear to someone in need. Their capacity for empathy without judgment easily attracts new friendships. While they typically avoid engaging in conflict, *SI's* are more than willing to mediate between others to restore peace.

SI's also add stability to professional environments by maintaining consistency through their methodical approach to completing tasks. Having built psychological safety around the status quo, *SI's* appreciate stable settings that feature long-term relationships and processes that do not require frequent and dramatic change.

SI's tend to overuse kindness, which can cause them to subjugate their own needs for the wants of others. Further, given their sensitive nature, *SI's* can become easily offended and can even hold grudges for long periods of time. *SI's* internalize stress and can act passive-aggressively.

CS – *The Perfectionist*
Logic and the need for accuracy drive the *CS*. After all, if it's not going to be done right, then why do it? The *C's* need for precision combined with the *S's* patience creates an individual with a strong quality focus. Essentially, *CS's* are perfectionists.

CS's think and plan ahead to avoid the unexpected. They make sure that ideas are carefully vetted by questioning assumptions, exploring alternatives, and considering worst-case scenarios. They thrive in settings in which they can receive and analyze tremendous amounts of information *before* reaching a conclusion or making a decision. *CS's* like to work within clearly defined boundaries and desired outcomes, but enjoy overcoming challenges through intense focus and persistence.

CS's need others who can see the big picture without getting bogged down in the details. Given their task-focused nature, *CS's* can also benefit from people who add positive energy to the environment, boosting morale and providing encouraging feedback.

CS's dislike working in settings that lack standard operating procedures. They are uncomfortable with sudden changes and loathe reckless risk-taking. The *CS's* fear of making a mistake can lead to time-consuming processes that strive for error-free outcomes.

In overuse, *CS's* can get so engrossed in their work that they may lose sight of the need to celebrate accomplishments and provide positive feedback to others. Under pressure, *CS's* can get caught up in "analysis paralysis" and create perfect plans, but remain fearful of taking action.

SC – The Loyalist

SC's naturally construct patterns that govern their world. This manifests in intense loyalty to people, brands, and procedures that have been proven successful over time. *SC's* build psychological safety around the status quo by establishing consistency in everything they do. They prefer predictability over rapid innovation and calm environments over fast-paced ones. As a result, *SC's* can get trapped in existing methodologies when new approaches might better capitalize on emerging opportunities.

SC's are modest about their abilities. While this can be an endearing trait in personal relationships, such humbleness can come across as meekness to more assertive styles. Their aversion to candor and constructive conflict can lead to passive-aggressive behaviors that prolong and intensify issues instead of solving them.

SC's shine in roles that demand both empathy and a curiosity for understanding why or how things have occurred. This allows them to be excellent listeners who can help *others* to work through issues. They avoid drawing attention to themselves and prefer quiet, intimate settings to large group gatherings. *SC's* like people, but tend to have just a few very close friends. They lead rich inner lives and often have more ideas than they actually express.

SC's dislike fast paced environments with rapid shifts in priorities. They are planners who don't want to be surprised. *SC's* don't like to say no, a trait that often leads to becoming overburdened with work, as they value both their commitment to the team and to quality results.

DC – The Driver

DC's seek to get things done with both urgency and complete accuracy. They have high expectations of themselves and others. The *Dominant* style is driven to achieve big goals while the *Conscientious* style insists that every step be well planned and properly executed. While the *D* loves to visualize the big picture and set broad goals that advance the cause, the *C* side of the same person will delve into the details, slowing down the urge to take big leaps. This internal struggle creates the constant push and pull between the desire for results and the desire for quality. *DC's* often believe that others will not strike the correct balance, and thus overburden themselves with work that could otherwise be delegated.

DC's thrive in environments where they have great autonomy to both set the agenda and help ensure that processes are followed through accurately. While *DC's* provide great contributions to projects large and small, they need people to help them appreciate the emotional or psychological impact that decisions might have on others. *DC's* are wired for task completion and goal acquisition, not nuanced communication skills or intuition about how people feel.

DC's are highly efficient and don't like it when others lack a sense of urgency for accomplishing goals and maintaining accuracy. They view work as the place to make things happen, not to engage in social or emotional commitments.

In overuse, *DC's* can become too demanding of both themselves and those around them. Left unchecked, their combination of *D*-inspired bluntness and *C*-oriented pickiness can add significant stress to the workplace.

CD – The Strategist
Like the *DC*, *CD's* focus on both accuracy and tangible outcomes. Their stronger *C* nature, however, brings diplomacy and patience to their *D* drive for accomplishment. *CD's* enjoy creating systems that will withstand rigorous quality standards while delivering significant results. They are talented planners but may overlook the human element that drives collaboration. *CD's* speak in specifics, preferring facts and examples over emotion and intuition to build their case. With their methodical nature and tendency to explore every option before arriving at a decision, *CD's* are often reluctant to make big, consequential decisions.

CD's tend to have a formal demeanor, display a limited range of facial expressions, and either avoid or minimize physical contact. In overuse, *CD's* can come across as cold, blunt, and detached in personal relationships. They are reluctant to discuss their feelings and tend to have a small, close circle of confidants.

DS/SD – The Activist

The *DS/SD* is one of the least prevalent styles. While their *D* nature focuses on results, their *S* nature cares about fairness and respect. This makes the *DS/SD* perfectly suited to fight for justice and equality. With tenacity and compassion, the *DS/SD* speaks up for those who are unwilling or unable. They are motivated by deeply held commitments and pursue their goals with persistence and devotion.

With the willpower of the *D* and the patience of the *S, Activists* display unwavering determination for their cause and have a strong sense of personal accountability.

While *DS/SD's* can sometimes appear to be detached from others, they are actually deeply emotional people. They are sensitive and can be easily offended, though they may camouflage it well.

It can be difficult to predict the reactions of *DS/SD* people, as sometimes they're in *D* mode—direct and results-oriented—and at other times, they're in *S* mode—caring and accommodating. They can be highly independent or may want to be a part of team striving to achieve their objectives. Regardless, *DS/SD's* are fiercely loyal to the people in their lives.

IC/CI – The Inventor

IC/CI is also a rare combination of styles within an individual. *Inventors* are superb at perceiving both the big picture and the details of complex projects. By recognizing interconnected systems, *IC/CI's* can link insights from one area to another and can predict the likelihood of success of a new endeavor very quickly.

Often it seems as though *IC/CI's* are painstakingly gathering tremendous amounts of data, while in other situations they seem to make snap judgments in rapid succession. This is because their voluminous *C* data is first stored, then accessed subconsciously through pattern recognition, culminating in what appears to be a flash moment of insight. However, because they quickly intuit solutions, *IC/CI's* can appear to be impulsive.

C's understand conventional wisdom. *I's* are willing to buck it. When you combine these traits, you get someone who has a thorough understanding of the past and a visionary picture of the future. This yields a resourceful innovator.

Inventors tend to be strong communicators, as *C's* measure their words carefully and *I's* are naturally skilled at influencing others. *IC/CI's* have to balance their social needs with their solitary needs. They love to be in groups, but must recharge their batteries alone. Their solitary "downtime" is often when they are most creative.

The History and Mystery of the Four Styles

Now that you better understand your behavioral style, let's place it in some context. The wisdom of styles has existed for millennia. Twenty-four hundred years ago, Hippocrates described four humours, and Aristotle, four elements. Variations of the four styles continued to appear over the centuries. In modern times, Carl Jung identified four functions; Eduard Spränger, four value attitudes; Erich Fromm, four orientations. Even Pavlov noted four temperaments—and he was studying dogs! William Marston designated four styles with words beginning with *D*, *I*, *S*, and *C,* and more than *50 million people* across the globe have taken profiles to identify their *DISC* styles.

So how is it that the styles have remained consistent for thousands of years, across continents and cultures, in people and in animals? The answer was finally revealed in the 1950s when landmark researchers observed that the four brain quadrants correspond to specific behavioral patterns.

Four brain quadrants—four styles. It's that simple. Our brain's hardwiring drives how we think, feel, and act, which in turn defines our style. Using the X-Factor graphic as a guide, if you're upper left-brained, you are *Dominant* like Dorian, the eagle. Upper right, you're *Interactive* like parrots Indy and Ivy. Lower right and you're *Supportive* like doves Samuel and Sarah. And lower left, you're *Conscientious* like the owls, Clark and Crystal.

If you're wondering whether the styles apply to real birds as well...they do. Evidently, birds are not so different from people after all.

People Reading

You enter a local restaurant and immediately notice your waitress's beaming grin and easy laugh. You watch how effortlessly she strikes up a conversation about last night's football game. She actually seems excited about what you've ordered and enthusiastically places it before you. She quickly greets another customer passing by, and all the while, she never stops smiling. You've likely identified your waitress as an *I*.

Wouldn't it be great if you could figure out someone's *DISC* style within a few minutes of meeting the person? Imagine how much easier it would be to communicate with your manager if you knew she was a *D*. How much more could you sell if you recognized your customer as an *I*? How would it impact your career if you realized that the person interviewing you was a *C*? And how much more effective would you be as a leader if you determined that you were managing a group of *S's?*

When observing others from a *DISC* perspective, each piece of the puzzle spontaneously assembles into an easily definable picture. No assessments are required. No lengthy analysis is needed. You can simply observe how they behave, how they move, and the way they speak, and it all comes together.

Tune into their words, tone, and body language. Are they animated or subdued? Rigid or relaxed? Observe their tone of voice. Is it upbeat and dynamic or soft and monotone? Do they speak quickly and spontaneously or slowly and measured? Do they make definitive statements that convey confidence or do they ask questions to assure understanding? Pay attention to how they listen. Are they empathetic listeners who validate emotions or impatient listeners who interrupt with their own ideas?

All of these characteristics are aspects of the behavioral style puzzle. The more you practice tuning into the pieces, the more adept you will become at identifying *DISC* styles. Most people find that after a few weeks of observing the styles of friends, family, or even characters on television shows or in movies, they can identify the styles of people they have just met—*in minutes, or even less.*

Consider the following observable signs of people with each of the four styles:

Dominant – The first sign that someone is a *D* is that they exude self-confidence. They stand tall, have a firm handshake, and maintain steady eye contact. The *D's* tone of voice is assertive and direct. They speak with such certainty that even when sharing a new idea, the *D* can come across as an expert. *D's* jump right to the matter at hand and dispense with the niceties. They call it like it is. Not to be bothered with fluff, they cut to the chase and ask for what they want. If you are providing too much detail, you may notice the *D's* impatience as they direct the conversation to the bottom line. You may also find that, at best, *D's* provide suggestions about how you should handle a situation or solve a problem. At worst, they impose their opinions or even their will upon you.

Interactive – The big smile, wide eyes, and hearty laugh that can fill a room are dead giveaways that you've encountered an *I*. In fact, you might find they laugh at their own jokes even more than their audience! They often use their full body to emphasize their excitement or to make a point, casually taking up lots of physical space. When *I's* speak, their tone ranges from happy to excited. Even small experiences are larger-than-life events for an *I*. If something is good, to an *I* it's *great!* If it's bad, it's *horrible.* Look for *I's* to comfortably start conversations with strangers, as they are energized by unfamiliar or large groups. They can build rapport easily, and within minutes they'll be talking to you as if they've known you for years. *I's* seem to have a story for every topic. At times it can even seem as if they need to "one up" whatever you have to say, but it's just the *I's* way of connecting with you.

Supportive – When you meet an *S*, you'll immediately notice that he or she radiates a sense of calm. The *S's* soft smile and gentle touch reveals a mild, sincere demeanor. Their tone is friendly and nurturing, and their volume is quiet as they rarely raise their voice, even when angry. They move deliberately and use a small range of gestures, careful not to take up too much physical space. *S's* shine in one-on-one interactions or in small, familiar groups. In these comfortable settings, they may be quite verbal and involved. However, in new or large groups, *S's* can easily be overlooked given their quiet, unobtrusive manner. When they sense that others are not well, you can see how effortlessly they tune into emotions and lend an empathetic ear.

Conscientious – You can immediately identify a strong *C* through their non-demonstrative, restrained movements. Their facial expression will often be flat, unemotional, and consistent. *C's* are sensitive to physical space. They're not likely to pat your back or offer a hug. They speak with their arms at their sides, rarely using them expressively as an *I* would. *C's* will typically make strong eye contact, but will rarely nod their head, smile, or give off cues that they agree or disagree with you, making them difficult to read. However, *C's* are patient listeners and will let you finish before they talk. And when they do, notice the level of detail they share, as well as the reasoning behind a decision or recommendation. *C's* favor logic over feelings and will relate even personal stories through facts and data. *C's* speak with intention, thus their words are measured and precise. Not comfortable with ambiguity, C's will ask lots of questions to ensure complete understanding.

Seven Transformative *DISC* Principles

In matters of style, swim with the current.
In matters of principle, stand like a rock.
—*Thomas Jefferson*

This section features seven *DISC* principles that will deepen your understanding of how to best internalize and apply the styles. Taken collectively, these principles provide a complete framework for understanding how the *DISC* can positively impact your life.

1. Understand your own style.
According to Aristotle, "Knowing yourself is the beginning of all wisdom." Why is this so important? Numerous studies indicate that individuals

who score high in self-awareness are happier and achieve greater success than those who lack it. Self-awareness enables people to build their lives around their strengths and better manage their challenges.

Example: Jennifer worked in a customer service department where she handled incoming calls. Her role involved patiently listening to customer issues, sympathizing with their perspective, and processing their complaints through a complex database. Before long, Jennifer felt as though she were repeating the same call over and over again. Although the job itself wasn't challenging, she found herself exhausted and stressed at the end of each day.

Following a *DISC* training program, Jennifer realized why she was so unhappy: She was a *D* working in an *S* job. Today, she is still at the company, but now thrives as a sales representative where she enjoys competitive goals and the personal initiative to accomplish them. In sales, Jennifer can take risks and use her direct and assertive nature to get results. Not only does she love her new position, but her company has benefitted twice: first by filling Jennifer's former job with an *S* who enjoys empathetically helping people, and again by placing Jennifer in a new style-appropriate role.

Have you ever known someone who consistently struggles with his or her career or has had many contentious relationships? Having worked with thousands of people from all walks of life, we see this on a regular basis. The common denominator is often that these individuals are out of touch with their own behavioral style. Consequently, they make critically important personal and professional decisions without considering how they are wired. Then they struggle.

When we truly know ourselves, we can make decisions that enable our strengths to shine.

2. Recognize the styles of others.

Sun Tzu said, "If you know the enemy and know yourself, you need not fear a hundred battles." So how do you identify someone else's style? Just ask yourself these questions: Are they fast-paced or even-paced? Are they outgoing or reserved? Are they detail-oriented or big-picture? Are they risk-takers or cautious? Are they planned or spontaneous? Each answer fills in a piece of the puzzle.

The more you practice reading people, the more intuitive it will become. In time, you'll be able to identify styles with ease. In fact, we'll bet that you've already developed people-reading skills. Let's give it a try. What styles best define the following people: Donald Trump, Robin Williams, Mother Theresa, and Bill Gates? Think about it for just a moment before you read on.

If you said *D, I, S,* and *C,* respectively, you're well on your way to recognizing the styles.

In our daily lives, this useful skill enables you to better leverage other people's strengths.

Example: Maria is a reserved, soft-spoken *S*. She needed to purchase a new car, but dreaded the idea of bargaining with a salesperson. While speaking with her sister, Jane, she realized that Jane's persuasive *I* style would be more adept at haggling for a great deal than her own *S* style. In the end, Jane got Maria a great price on the car and was even energized by the experience. Maria was relieved and grateful that she didn't have to negotiate the deal.

By recognizing the styles of others, you can leverage their strengths to supplement things that you find challenging, and vice versa. In doing so, you utilize the power of the *DISC* styles to create true partnerships. Whether it's a coworker, spouse, child, or friend, understanding others is the foundation for strong relationships, better results, and a more fulfilling life.

3. Think about style when establishing expectations.

We view the world through the lens of our behavioral style. Consequently, our expectations are driven by our own style rather than by the styles of others. We expect others to like what we like and need what we need. We assume people can do what we can do and will react as we would react. Further, we assume that the people in our lives understand our needs and will fulfill them...*without our having to express them.* After all, shouldn't they already *know* what we want?

Example: Jasmine and Steve worked in adjacent cubicles at a major bank. The problem was that Steve played his music too loudly...or at least that's what Jasmine thought. A strong *D,* Steve assumed that if Jasmine didn't like his music, she'd pop her head over his cubicle and say so. But she never mentioned it. In reality, Jasmine, a strong *S,* had been stewing over his apparent lack of respect. "He *must* know it bothers me," she thought, "but he obviously doesn't care."

Weeks passed and Jasmine grew increasingly annoyed. She complained to her husband, who suggested that she talk to Steve, but she was reluctant. "He should know better and just stop playing the music!" she protested. Another week passed, and finally Jasmine couldn't take it anymore and decided to give Steve a piece of her mind. "How do you concentrate with that music?" she asked, to which he replied, "I like it."

This only frustrated Jasmine even more.

Both Jasmine and Steve were trapped in their styles, unable to see the other's perspective. Steve thought that if the music bothered Jasmine, she would just tell him. And why not? For a *D,* it's no big deal to address issues directly because *D's* don't perceive direct communication as conflict. Instead, they see it as simply making a request. And talking about it is merely a conversation, not an argument.

As for Jasmine, her *S*-guided sensitivity couldn't relate to how Steve was behaving because she would never do such a thing. Yet she was not about to start a conflict with someone...over music, no less! Besides, in her mind, she *did* address it with him, and furthermore, she didn't want him to feel attacked.

Of course, Jasmine's indirect request lacked the assertiveness that would spur Steve to act. *D's* are direct about their needs and expect others to be direct as well. They don't perceive a direct statement as an attack.

Unrealistic expectations lead to disappointment, poor results, ineffective decision making, increased conflict, and resentment. Fortunately, style awareness allows you to establish *realistic* expectations. By understanding your own style, recognizing the styles of others, and establishing expectations based upon what *others* need, both parties are likely to get their needs met.

4. Consider intention, not just behavior.
We judge ourselves by our intentions and others by their actions. Better understanding intentions of others prevents misinterpretation and takes the sting out of actions that could otherwise feel hurtful.

Example: One morning, Jake, a marketing executive, called George, his associate, into his office to delegate a critical project. Following their 90-minute meeting, Jake, true to his *C* style, felt confident that George had all of the information he needed to be successful. George, an *I*, felt quite differently. Jake had restricted him with so many processes and details that there was no room for George to think for himself or create something new. He left feeling frustrated and resentful.

"Why doesn't Jake just do it himself?" George thought. "After a year in this job, he still doesn't trust me or else he would have simply handed off the project and let me figure it out. What a micromanager." Soon after, George began looking for another job.

What happened? By not understanding his boss's style, George incorrectly assumed Jake's intent. In actuality, Jake trusted George completely. That's why he selected him to lead such an important project. His goal was simply to ensure that George had all of the tools he needed to be successful. Had Jake recognized George's style, he would have simply stated the goal, outlined the project, and let George move forward as he saw fit.

As for George, if he understood that Jake's intention was really just to be helpful, he wouldn't have felt micromanaged and mistrusted.

The *DISC* model is a powerful tool for understanding intentions and recognizing the source of behaviors that might otherwise irritate you. However, just because you understand someone's intent doesn't mean that you should tolerate disrespect, poor quality, or failure to achieve results. Positive intentions don't justify using style as a weapon. Jake shouldn't excuse his behavior by saying, "I'm a *C* and that means I provide a lot of information and structure. Deal with it."

People usually aim to satisfy *their own* needs, not to push *your* buttons. In other words, they do things *for* themselves, not *against* you. So the next time you experience a difficult conversation or engage in conflict, consider that you may be misreading the other person's intention.

5. Use your strengths, but don't overuse them.

Too much of a good thing is *not* a good thing. When a strength is overused, it becomes a weakness. And while each of the *DISC* styles is inherently positive, when carried to an extreme, any style can become a disadvantage.

<u>Example</u>: Kate, a strong *C,* walked through her front door with six bags of groceries and a plan. It was 9:00 a.m. and eighteen guests would be arriving later that afternoon for their annual holiday dinner.

Although Kate had several days to prepare for the event, she used a good deal of that time to plan the menu and identify tasks that needed to be accomplished to get the house in order. When she was finally ready to put her plan into action, she had a long list of to-dos and little time to implement them.

As soon as she reached the kitchen, Kate's husband, Mark—an intuitive *I*—immediately sensed her stress level and offered, "Relax, babe. It's just my parents and my sisters' families. What can we do to help?"

Kate was already feeling overwhelmed. In the past, she had delegated tasks to Mark, but they were rarely done according to her standards and it usually meant that she had to do them herself anyway. She was reluctant to take him up on his offer to assist, but with so much to be done she asked him to set the dining room table. Off he went. A few minutes later Mark returned with a cheerful, "What's next?"

Skeptical that he could finish so quickly, Kate went in to inspect, sighed, and simply said, "Don't worry, I'll do it."

"But it's already done," Mark thought to himself as he raised his hands in confusion. Evidently, he had used the wrong tablecloth and napkins for this holiday, put the water glasses on the incorrect side, placed trivets in the wrong places, and didn't consider that two of the kids shouldn't receive the fine china.

"They won't care," comforted Mark. "It's my family. This looks fine."

"Just straighten up the living room and I'll fix the dining room."

By 1:30 p.m., Kate became more tense as she sensed the impending arrival of her guests. There was still much to be done: Rosemary chicken, sweet potatoes, and asparagus in the oven, a pot of home-made tomato bisque on the stovetop, and a half-completed salad on the counter.

Mark, trying to stay out of the line of fire, approached the kitchen to check Kate's progress. "Hey, we're almost ready," he declared.

"Almost ready?" Kate shot back with a glare. "Do you know how much more we have to do? All of the food needs to be placed in the right dishes... the counters need to be wiped down...the living room is still a mess..." and the list went on.

By the time the guests arrived, all of the pieces were in place. Afterwards, Mark's mother commented, "Everything was wonderful. What a lovely evening."

However, as Kate reflected on the night, her stomach tightened. She had forgotten to serve one of the desserts, the soup was a bit salty, and she failed to replace the tablecloth that Mark incorrectly put on the dining room table. "If only Mark would have been more helpful," she thought.

Kate's *C* enabled her to organize a beautiful dinner. However, the tight deadline caused by her excessive planning drove Kate to overuse her style and she became stressed and inflexible. By seeking perfection, she elevated both her and her husband's stress level over an event that was supposed to be enjoyable. Instead of accepting help to reduce her stress, Kate alienated her partner by being overly critical. In the end the meal was a success, but at a high emotional cost.

While some people overuse their style on a regular basis, most of us over-do it during times of stress or uncertainty. Style excess can also be driven by emotionally charged situations or dysfunctional relationships. But no matter the cause, too much of any style creates added stress for everyone involved. Here's a brief overview of the shadow side of style:

When *D*'s overuse their style, their interpersonal skills take a back seat to achieving results. Their directness turns blunt, abrasive, and insensitive. In the extreme, the *D's* take-charge mind-set becomes overly demanding and domineering. Their confidence degenerates to stubborn, closed-minded arrogance as they steamroll over anyone who interferes with achieving their objective.

When *I's* overuse their style, their optimism can lead to unrealistic, impractical ideas, where gut feelings take precedence over reality and their enthusiasm comes across as superficial. Lacking essential facts and details, *I's* can lean on exaggeration and manipulation to persuade others. Under stress, *I's* often appear disorganized, manage their time poorly, and simply try to talk their way out of difficult situations instead of executing the plan.

When *S's* overuse their style, their need for harmony leads to an avoidance of difficult conversations and healthy conflict. Their deep comfort with the status quo can also lead to complacency and a resistance to change. This causes them to become passive and dependent. When *S's* don't get their needs met, they can become resentful and develop a victim mentality. In overuse mode, *S's* simply wait for instruction from others, and therefore appear fearful and unsure of themselves.

When *C's* overuse their style, their drive for quality and structure degenerates into perfectionism. They become so picky and critical that nothing meets their standards or gets accomplished. This makes them seem indecisive and rigid. Their need to question everything can lead to pessimism and resistance to new ideas. Their intense focus on the task can blind them to healthy delegation opportunities and place significant pressure on *C's* to do everything themselves.

6. Apply the right style at the right time.
In the fable, Xavier understood that adaptability was the key to survival. Being a chameleon, he adjusted

naturally to his surroundings and connected with everyone. In our own lives, we too can reap the benefits of accurately reading people and situations and then tapping into the right style at the right time. When we don't, we fail to meet objectives and are surprised by how others perceive us.

<u>Example</u>: It was a big day for Spencer, who was about to lead a sales presentation that could result in significant revenues for his firm. Joanne, the company president, greeted him with a quick handshake and said, "Tell me about your company and what you can do for us."

Spencer opened with his professional background and a brief overview of his company. His primary objective was to establish rapport. After all, his strength was in building relationships.

It didn't take long for Spencer to discover that he had grown up just a town away from Joanne. They swapped childhood stories and reminisced about the good old days.

Next, Spencer unveiled a dazzling PowerPoint presentation that featured eye-popping graphics and a compelling vision. Joanne smiled throughout. Spencer closed by reassuring Joanne that his company had worked on many projects of this magnitude and that they would do a great job if selected. Driving back to the office, he felt he had made a strong impression.

One week later, Spencer was devastated to learn that a competitor had won the account. Joanne remarked to Spencer's boss that while he gave an energetic and appealing presentation, it didn't inspire her confidence that the job would get done. She wanted steak and all he delivered was sizzle. Joanne had wanted to learn more about his company could do, not about Spencer.

Spencer's mistake: He treated Joanne like a fellow *I* when she was, in fact, a *D*. His failure to read her correctly and adapt to her style doomed his success.

Most people have one style that they use too often and one that they don't use enough. Spencer failed to flex his *D* in order to connect with Joanne, and as a result, she didn't get her needs met. Each style is needed at one time or another. The key is to be flexible enough to exhibit the right style at the right time.

7. Treat others how *they* need to be treated, not how *you* need to be treated (the "Home Rule"). The Golden Rule—treating others the way *you* want to be treated—can be traced back to a wide range of world cultures and religions. The Golden Rule is the foundation for meaningful relationships and cohesive societies when expressed through timeless values such as honesty, integrity, respect, and fairness.

However, as we learned in principle #5 about overuse, anything carried to an extreme can become a detriment. The Golden Rule is so ingrained in our thinking that we apply it universally...and that gets us into trouble. The "Home Rule" that we learned in the birds' story—treat others the way *they* need to be treated—is a much more effective strategy when it comes to communication and working together to achieve shared outcomes.

Example: Bashir, VP of Information Technology at a large insurance company, sought to roll out a major software upgrade throughout the organization. A year prior, however, his predecessor had struggled mightily with a very similar project, leading to cost overruns and disapproval from senior management. Working with the same staff, whose memory of the previous debacle was still fresh, Bashir needed this project to run smoothly.

To achieve a high level of buy-in, Bashir resisted a natural tendency to communicate solely within his *S* style. Instead, he intuitively recognized the need to connect with the full range of styles represented by his staff. One department at a time, Bashir gathered employees to explain the new system, fluidly adapting to each of the four styles like a chameleon.

When Bashir opened with, "Here's the executive summary," he immediately captured the *D's* attention by providing the bottom-line impact. For the *I's*, he turned on the enthusiasm: "You're going to love this system. It's cutting-edge...better than anything you've ever seen!" They left feeling excited and eager to use the new system. Bashir validated the S's perspective by revealing his own resistance to change: "I realize that this represents a big transition and that might be stressful, so we'll be offering support throughout the process to allay concerns as they arise." To address the C's priorities, who were feverishly taking notes on the PowerPoint handout, Bashir spoke in a measured tone and laid out a comprehensive, coherent plan. He encouraged them to ask questions and patiently answered each one. They emerged confident that the new system was well thought-out.

Bashir left each meeting feeling a bit drained, as he had worked outside of his style for much of the time. But it was worth it. He had created an army of change agents who had bought into the new system. After meeting with Bashir, the D's got the bottom line, the I's were energized, the S's were reassured, and the C's got the specifics they needed. The upgrade was implemented with great ease and minimal stress for everyone involved.

As Danish physicist Niels Bohr noted, "The opposite of a profound truth may well be another profound truth." So it is with the Golden Rule and the Home Rule. Both reinforce the notion that we should honor people for who they are and respect their needs and differences.

Part III

Unleashing the Power of *DISC*

Steps for Reaching Your Highest Potential

> Weakness fixing is damage control,
> but it is not development.
> And damage control can prevent failure, but it will
> never elevate you to excellence.
> —*Marcus Buckingham and Donald O. Clifton*

Given that overused strengths become liabilities, the key to personal growth lies not in fixing weaknesses, but rather in toning down the overuse of our strengths. As the Oracle at Delphi noted 2,500 years ago, "Everything in moderation."
Toning down your predominant style allows your underused styles to emerge. The following strategies will help you minimize the overuse of your style.

Those with a strong *Dominant* style may need to tone down:

- *Directness* – D's have a thin filter between thinking and speaking. This leads to directness that can be perceived as blunt insensitivity. Ask more questions and soften your tone.
- *Fast pace* – When D's are too hasty, they can make poor decisions and become reckless. Slow down and think things through.
- *Reactive nature* – In a crisis, D's can save the day with their quick thinking and reactive nature.

However, everything is not an emergency. Exercise patience and anticipate how your words or decisions might impact others.

- *Drive* – An intense drive for results enables *D's* to achieve great things. It can also lead to high levels of personal stress. Take time to relax and enjoy the fruits of your labor.

- *Ego* – Confidence is a good thing, but when overused, it comes across as arrogance. Your unwavering conviction can shut down the ideas of others, especially if your mind is already made up. Recognize the abilities and contributions of others.

- *Powerful stature* – *D's* embody power and authority, but in overuse, this can be intimidating, preventing the best idea from emerging. Be aware of your body language. Smile and make eye contact.

- *Seeking Authority* – *D's* like to be directive, but this can limit opportunities for others, creating dependencies instead of multiplying the capabilities of teammates. Allow others to take the lead, delegate more, and share decision making.

- *Risk-taking* – *D's* take big risks to get big rewards. Sometimes the most effective approach is a tried-and-true method. You don't always have to reinvent the wheel.

Those with a strong *Interactive* style may need to tone down:

- *Talkativeness* – If there's one behavior that truly characterizes the *I* style, it's the tendency to talk...*a lot*. And when other people are speaking, *I's* are likely thinking about what they're going to say next. Ask more questions and show more interest in what others have to say.

- *Optimism* – The *I's* tendency to see the best in everyone and everything can lead to unrealistic expectations. Develop the objectivity to view things as they are, not as you want them to be.

- *Spontaneity* – *I's* enjoy living in the moment. Sometimes, this results in a lack of planning and thinking things through. Consider several options before acting.

- *Multitasking* – *I's* desire variety and stimulation. This can lead to working on too many things at once, such as checking email while talking on the phone. Complete one task before starting another one.

- *Casualness* – *I's* enjoy building relationships. Consequently, they can come across as too friendly in formal situations. Recognize that certain environments require a more professional demeanor.

- *Enthusiasm* – *I's* exude positive energy and excitement for everything they do. Their bubbly nature can annoy others who want to see results, focus on details, or prefer a more tranquil, or serious, environment. Stay focused on the task, not just the *idea* of the task.

- *Unstructured approach* – *I's* seek freedom from constraints, as this allows their creativity to flow in new directions. However, their nonconformity can stray too far from accepted norms and lead them to break the rules. Recognize the importance of following established procedures.

- *Big-picture thinking* – The ability to see the forest from the trees enables *I's* to generate innovative solutions to problems. Yet this visionary focus can lead to overlooking key details and making mistakes. Take time to consider all of the facts before making decisions.

Those with a strong *Supportive* style may need to tone down:

- *Harmony* – *S's* thrive in settings that are free of conflict and discontent. They can shy away from potential disagreements that could lead to innovation, better results, or higher levels of trust. Engage in candid conversations that address your concerns.

- *Laid-back nature* – *S's* tend to go with the flow, so as not to make waves. And while they may have strong opinions, they may not voice them and thus appear unsure or indifferent. Speak up and stand up for what you believe in.

- *Steadiness* – *S's* seek to maintain the status quo. This can lead to a lack of innovation and an aversion to change. Go beyond the norm by trying new things and experimenting with different approaches.
- *Accommodation* – *S's* want to please others and thus find it difficult to say no. Assert and respect your own priorities.
- *Self-sufficiency* – While *S's* are great team players, they often take on too much work, as they don't want to impose on others. Delegate if your plate is full.
- *Followership* – *S's* don't often gravitate to roles of authority. If you feel passionately about a cause or project, take control and lead.
- *Security* – *S's* tend to go with what's tried and true. Try new things, even if you're a little scared.
- *Methodical nature* – *S's* tend to work within pre-established procedures. Their step-by-step approach can make it difficult to deal with the unexpected. Be ready and willing to act without a plan.

Those with a strong *Conscientious* style may need to tone down:
- *Logic* – *C's* need tangible verification before making a decision. But sometimes decisions must be made without all the facts. Trust your instincts, even when lacking all of the data to back you up.

- *Criticalness* – C's have high standards. When applied to people, this can lead to judgment and a lack of acceptance. Establish realistic expectations for the work of others.
- *Perfectionism* – The desire for accuracy enables C's to engineer quality results. However, perfection is time-consuming and can lead to ideal plans with little or no action analysis. Accept that in some situations, good enough may well be…good enough.
- *Task-focus* – C's tend to put their energy into getting things done rather than on living in the moment. This can lead to high levels of stress. Explore the benefits of play and do things just for the fun of it.
- *Sarcasm* – C's tend to be uncomfortable with interpersonal conflict. When situations get emotionally charged, they tend to use sarcasm to indirectly raise concerns and mask attacks with humor. Address concerns directly with others.
- *Rationality* – C's respond to situations from the head rather than the heart. They focus on facts and disregard that others are driven by emotions and intuition. Recognize that decisions aren't just about logic, and some people do things just because it "feels" right.
- *Self-reliance* – C's set high standards and follow processes. Sometimes, their standards are so high and the processes are so complicated that they

themselves are the only ones who can complete the task. Recognize that there may be more than one way to solve a problem, and tap into the strengths of others.

- *Pride* – *C's* take great pride in their work. This can cause them to associate the quality of what they do with their self-worth. Accept yourself for who you *are* rather than what you *do*.

DISC in the Work Environment

The degree to which people like their jobs is largely a function of the corporate culture in which they work. People spend a significant percentage of their waking lives at work, so matching work environment with style can lead to greater job satisfaction and a more rewarding career. While no setting will likely satisfy every want or need, there's a lot to be said for understanding which kinds of environments bring out our best.

What follows are optimal work environments and general job characteristics that match each style. _Dominant style:_ *D's* thrive in environments that value big-picture ideas and high levels of accountability for getting things done. Someone high in *D* energy will thrive in a culture where setting ambitious goals and aggressively pursuing results take precedence over playing it safe. *D's* prefer settings where candor is considered healthy and constructive conflict is welcomed. An environment that encourages competition can bring out the best in the *D's* performance.

While *D's* often strive for bold strategies that are well executed, they need to be supported by others who will carefully consider the impact of their decisions on the people involved and the organization itself. An environment that supports quick decision making and a willingness to break new ground will suit *D's* well.

Interactive style: Given that *I's* are enthusiastic, optimistic, and upbeat, they thrive in high-energy, positive work environments. A workplace with low morale can have a particularly devastating effect on the *I's* job satisfaction. The *I's* desire to talk and contribute necessitates an atmosphere that encourages group interaction. *I's* thrive when empowered with freedom and flexibility. Jobs that require the frequent juggling of responsibilities are well suited to an *I's* thirst for variety and spontaneity. In fact, multitasking keeps the *I's* mind active and engaged.

A "command and control" manager will not bring out the best in an *I*. Likewise, highly structured and formalized settings can seriously stifle an *I's* talent for motivating others and stimulating innovation.

Supportive style: *S's* are driven by their need for stability. As such, they prefer calm and steady work environments. *S's* will typically experience significant levels of stress in settings where constant change is the norm.

Seeking harmony in all of their relationships, *S's* thrive in collaborative workplaces in which people genuinely support each other. *S's* like to work with those who are sensitive about how workplace changes affect the emotional needs of employees. To an *S,* a harmonious environment brings out the best in everyone. *S's* dislike when people are domineering or excessively blunt. An overly candid culture can cause an *S* to become offended by the words and actions of others and thus lower overall job satisfaction.

Conscientious style: *C's* are detail-oriented and logical, and have a relentless need for accuracy. If a culture doesn't reward quality, *C's* will not be satisfied with their work. As such, they thrive in formalized settings with definable standards and expectations. A highly collaborative, free-flowing, and unstructured workplace would not be optimal for strong *C's,* as they prefer to work independently and need quiet to think.

C's also require ample time for analysis before arriving at a concrete conclusion. A fast-paced atmosphere where people spontaneously make decisions based upon intuition and gut feeling would be unsettling and disruptive. *C's* need to understand the logic behind decisions, and therefore will thrive in settings in which managers provide rationale and an abundance of information.

The right style of work environment will supercharge your skills and become a reliable source of vitality in your life. The wrong environment will drain your energy reserves and lead to much stress and conflict for you and your coworkers. So, when looking for a job, remember to consider workplace culture as one of the key criteria to determine if a job or company is right for you. And if you're a manager who helps to create the environment for your staff, try to factor in styles when dealing with each individual.

Tapping the Power of Style in Teams

While leading team building programs for more than half of the Fortune 100 companies, we have seen the direct impact that style has on success. Many teams have effectively navigated through the challenges inherent in teams that contain multiple styles, while other teams have worked through the difficulties of having all of its members with the same style.

No matter what the composition of your team, style can be its greatest asset or a hidden and devastating liability.

When most teams are formed, managers give significant consideration to the skills that will be required to deliver results. Selection criteria typically include an individual's background, work experience, education, and technical skills.

Example: Craig is a manager who is putting together a team for an important project. While evaluating bios and resumes of potential team members, Craig notes that Ruben has worked on a similar project, so his expertise will be valuable. Keiko's product knowledge and experience with the target market will be critical. Julia understands the technology and systems that will be needed throughout the process, and Phillip's project management skills will help keep the group on track. Voilà—the perfect team.

However, like many managers, Craig overlooked style as a key variable that drives success. As such, he failed to consider *how* they would interact, which is just as important as, if not more important than, *what* they know. While this team looks great on paper, without style awareness it has the potential to dissolve into an underperforming, stressed-out group of people who are a "team" in name alone.

Consider Craig's team if it had members of all different styles

At their first meeting, Ruben, a *D,* wants the group to start tackling the most difficult challenge: "Once we get this part of the project behind us, we'll have made solid progress." Keiko, an *I,* wants to begin with something engaging and easily accomplished: "Why start with the hardest part of the project? Let's build momentum by beginning with something we can all do well." Julia, a *C*, wants to organize the entire project before they start: "We shouldn't do anything until we have a comprehensive plan." And Phillip, an *S*, just wants to smooth over the initial dissention: "Let's take a step back. We're not going to get anything done unless we all get along."

If this group fails to recognize and respect the styles of others, these differences, while small at this stage of the game, can morph into serious impediments to teamwork as the project moves forward.

Consider a team whose members all share the same style

In addition to teams where members all have different styles, we have worked with many teams that consist of all one style. For example, a group that specializes in software development would most likely be *C's*, whereas a marketing group may contain many *I's*. A senior team of supply chain executives may very well be all *D's*, while a team of nurses may reflect a strong *S* composition.

You may be thinking, "What's wrong with that? After all, wouldn't communication be easier if we all had the same style and spoke the same language?" Perhaps, but when everyone shares a similar profile, the strengths of that style get magnified. Recall that strengths overused become weaknesses. Moreover, the absence of the three remaining styles would create triple the potential for blind spots. Consider a team with:

All D's – This team's primary focus is on achieving results—*immediate results.* They think fast and act even faster. The *D* team is not concerned with "the way we used to do things" or with creating extensive processes. They're willing to take risks and may sacrifice quality for speed. For a group of *D's,* action always trumps inaction and problems that pop up will be fixed as they go along. Another hallmark of a *D* team is that conflict is practically encouraged as team members prize directness and candor over tact and diplomacy.

<u>Potential blind spots for a team of *D's* include</u>:
1. Lack of detailed planning coupled with impulsive decision making that can lead to poor outcomes
2. Failure to anticipate process or procedural issues
3. Failure to get buy-in and support on decisions
4. Power struggles as every team member feels he or she should be in charge
5. Offending people on other teams, as their "pull no punches" approach is respected on their team, but may be considered insulting by others

All I's – Morale is sky-high with this configuration. Positive reinforcement and high-fives keep the momentum going. This team always looks on the bright side. People respect each other and prop each other up when things go wrong. Planning? No time. "We just go for it!" they declare proudly. "Don't worry. It'll work out." Processes and systems? Too constraining. This team likes to respond to sudden changes on the fly. Collaboration within this group is so high that everyone knows what all the others are thinking...about *everything*.

<u>Potential blind spots for a team of *I's* include</u>:
1. Lack of follow-through on commitments
2. Poor time management
3. Inability to drill down to the details of a project
4. Overly optimistic forecasts
5. Lack of desire to address performance issues
6. A shared assumption that others will react with their level of enthusiasm
7. Impulsive decision making as opposed to thinking through potential consequences

All S's – The S team is grounded in harmony. Respect and loyalty are of the utmost importance. In such a peaceful climate, conflict is painstakingly avoided. As a result, issues and concerns are often internalized rather than dealt with. The environment is casual and personal. Everyone knows about each other's children, spouses, pets, and interests. Meetings are cordial and there is rarely any dissention. Team members support each other whenever possible. If something goes wrong, someone will be there to rescue you, even at the expense of his or her own priorities. As for processes, they will remain consistent over long periods of time.

Potential blind spots for a team of *S's* include:

1. Working on the first idea proposed, as opposed to the best idea, which can only emerge by asking difficult questions
2. An unwillingness to take risks, either as a compelling need or to seize a unique opportunity
3. A tendency to over-personalize office relationships
4. Gossip can become rampant as people are interested in the personal lives of others and use the grapevine as a substitute for addressing difficult issues directly with the person involved
5. Minimal conflict reinforces the status quo and thus leads to minimal innovation

All C's – Quality is the name of the game for this team. An intensive focus on details and precision drive excellence, but getting there may take time. Their motto could be "We may not be the fastest, but we get it right the first time because we think things through *before* we act." This team can be relied upon to stick to pre-established procedures. Even their meetings follow a predetermined structure and adhere to the schedule. This team doesn't waste time with idle chatter, as they are highly focused on the work at hand.

Potential blind spots for a team of *C's* include:
1. Inability to grasp the big picture by getting caught up in the details
2. An overabundance of processes and quality control can slow down the process
3. Taking too long to make decisions and getting trapped in "analysis paralysis"
4. Lack of flexibility can cause inefficiency
5. Hyper-focusing on the task can lead to inattentiveness in creating an engaging work environment with high levels of job satisfaction

Consider a team that is missing one of the styles
While some teams are comprised of all one style, other teams can pay the price for missing a single style. This type of team may fail to adapt to the right style at the right time. Lacking one of the styles can cause blind spots that negatively impact the team environment and the results. Imagine a team without each style:

Without D's – This group occasionally will get off track and lose sight of the goal. They may have difficulty maintaining focus on their primary objective, as there is no *D* to keep the big picture in mind. Further, *D's* add a level of candor and they "call it like it is." This group may not be willing to address the *real* issues and thus may have difficulty realizing their ultimate vision.

Without I's – Sometimes things don't go as planned. Without *I's*, who have a way of loosening tension with humor, this team may experience more stress during times of adversity or high-volume periods. Morale will likely be lower without a few optimistic *I's* around.

Without S's – Minus the *S's*, conflict is sure to be more frequent and longer lasting, as there is no one to smooth over issues and mediate disagreements. In the absence of the *S's* calming energy, this environment is likely to feel more chaotic. *S's* are the glue that holds teams together, and without them, teamwork can come apart.

Without C's – Lacking *C's* to play the devil's advocate role, this team may not think things through before taking action. This team may also lack repeatable processes that drive consistent outcomes. Overall, without *C's*, quality may well suffer.

Steps to tapping the power of style in teams
By making the *DISC* a part of a team's everyday life, style can become a key driver of success and overall job satisfaction. Here are five key steps to making the most of your team.

1. **Educate people about the styles.** Devote time to teaching team members about the *DISC* styles to increase self-awareness, build acceptance, generate trust, and improve overall team effectiveness.
2. **Identify the style of each team member.** Create a chart that lists each person and his or her *DISC* style, and make sure that everyone knows the style of every member.
3. **Consider the team dynamic that is created by the combination of styles.** Note whether any particular style is in abundance or lacking.
4. **Identify group strengths and blind spots.** Every mix of styles creates a unique set of strengths and challenges. Take steps to ensure that the team capitalizes on its strengths while minimizing the possibility that potential blind spots become realized.
5. **Create a strategy to address style imbalances within the team.** Sometimes, the simple awareness that a style is in abundance allows team members to consciously notice

when the negative overuse of behaviors is leading to poor results or a de-motivating work environment. When a team realizes that a style is underrepresented, the members should proactively engage the strengths of the missing style. Some teams may even choose to fill a style gap with a new team member. Either way, teams that understand their *DISC* style makeup can utilize style to drive, rather than inhibit, success.

DISC for Teaching and Coaching

Whether you're teaching children or adults in a classroom, coaching players on a sports team, or providing feedback to people at work, *DISC* can be a powerful addition to the educator's toolbox.

Most of us enjoyed a teacher or two who had a lasting and positive effect on our lives. They seemed to intuitively *get* what we were about, and as a result, brought out our best. Other teachers seemed to be exasperated at our very presence and quite possibly left us feeling inadequate.

If you ask one hundred teachers if they adapt their teaching style to suit the student, you'll most likely receive one hundred "Yes!" responses. In fact, most teachers *are* taught to consider the learning styles of their students. However, educators typically define learning styles as auditory (learning by listening), visual (learning by seeing), or kinesthetic (learning by doing). Teachers generally aren't taught to consider the *DISC* styles of their students.

Example: Ms. Brown is a dedicated and diligent teacher who possesses strong communication skills. She uses a wide array of tools, such as well-organized handouts, tried-and-true lesson plans, innovative Internet-based videos, and interactive exercises. Sounds great, doesn't it? Really, who *wouldn't* want Ms. Brown at the head of their third-grader's class? Well, Austin's parents, that's who. Austin is a spirited, creative *I*-style kid who likes to do things *his* way.

One day, Ms. Brown asked her students to draw a figure inside a square. Austin's idea was too large to fit in the square, so he continued to draw on the back of the paper, nearly filling it up. Austin was proud of his work. Ms. Brown considered Austin's picture to be original, but not what the instructions had specified. Austin received a low grade. When he asked Ms. Brown why, her response was curt: "You didn't follow the instructions, Austin."

This pattern played out time and again throughout the school year. As a result, Austin became increasingly disheartened. In fact, he became quite confused when he remembered Ms. Rodriguez, his second-grade teacher, who was a big fan of his creativity and unconventional approaches.

Ms. Brown failed to appreciate Austin's style and missed a golden opportunity to celebrate and encourage Austin's creativity while simultaneously conveying the importance of following directions. Austin now understands the consequences of not following Ms. Brown's instructions; however, this "learning" cost him his motivation. This will not make Ms. Brown's job any easier going forward.

Educating with *DISC*

Understanding and applying the *DISC* model could turn these situations around. Teachers and coaches may erroneously assume that "people want to be taught how I want to be taught" (the Golden Rule), but the wiser course of action is to use the Home Rule: Treat others as *they* need to be treated. Use the following guidelines to increase your effectiveness and make a significant difference in people's lives:

Understand your own behavioral style. *Knowing your own style* is the foundational step for teaching others. It ensures that educators will not impose their own style on students and team members.

<u>D instructors</u> may cover material too fast and fail to provide information and examples from multiple perspectives. Their bottom-line approach may not provide context for the

new knowledge, and they may not be sensitive to the emotional needs of the students.

I instructors may create a fun learning environment, but not provide enough structure for those students who need it. They may not teach with a step-by-step logical order that both *C's* and *S's* require.

C instructors may not provide enough flexibility for "free-thinking" students. They may also restrict a fun learning environment that *I's* thrive in.

S instructors may be too accommodating and not push students beyond self-imposed limitations. The *S* teacher may not challenge the *D's* enough or go fast enough for *I's*.

Recognize the styles of the students. Every lesson needs to be taught such that no matter what *your* style is as the educator or coach, the information is conveyed with an understanding of the styles of the *learners*. Factors to consider include pacing and repetition, opportunities for independent and group work, the quantity of information that is shared, and the type of methods used to convey that information. By considering *DISC* style, you give all of the students the chance to participate, learn, and succeed.

When instructing *D's* — Explain the reason for the lesson upfront and link it to the world around them or their specific situation. Provide a snapshot of learning points right at the beginning.

When instructing *I's* — Make the learning fun, engaging, and interactive. Use a variety of teaching methods and allow for spontaneity and active engagement.

When instructing *S's* — Relate the topic back to the *S's* personal life and experiences. Make the learning emotionally meaningful to the learner. Be sensitive to the *S's* reserved nature and don't put him or her on the spot.

When instructing *C's* — Provide detail, structure, and logical sequencing to the lesson. Back up assertions with facts and be prepared to answer many questions.

No matter who you're teaching or where you're teaching it, *DISC* can make the difference between being a mediocre teacher and being a transformative figure in a person's life.

Better Parenting with *DISC*
We all know that children don't come with instruction manuals. However, one of the toughest lessons of being a parent may be to simply *let our children*

teach us who they are and how best to raise them. Parents must accept that they can impart their values, teach proper etiquette, and share valuable life skills, but they cannot determine their child's behavioral style for them. They are who they are.

<u>Example</u>: Brandon is an eight-year-old boy with strong *C* tendencies. He's introverted, independent, and asks lots of questions to better understand the world around him. He enjoys playing piano and collecting rocks and fossils. He has never liked playing team sports, though he enjoys the martial arts, as it gives him the opportunity to master a skill without having to compete with a team full of people. He has one close friend, which suits him just fine.

Brandon's father, a high *D*, and his mother, a high *I*, worry about him. "He doesn't have many friends," frets his mother. "He doesn't go outside and play basketball like the other boys," says his father.

Every day, Brandon's mother encourages him to reach out to other kids in the neighborhood, but Brandon just wants to play the piano or reach the next level in his video game. When his father gets home and sees other kids playing basketball, he not only "encourages" Brandon to play, but also shouts loudly from the sidelines, "Get in there! Go for the ball!"

Brandon's parents only want "what's best" for their child. His father wants him to taste success by being more competitive. His mother wants him to be more social. This, of course, is no surprise, coming from *D* and *I* parents.

However, the message that Brandon is receiving loud and clear is that he needs to change his personality to please his parents. "I don't even like basketball," Brandon thinks to himself, "especially the way my dad wants me to play. I see my friends at school. At home I'm cool with doing my own thing. They just don't get me."

Parents need to clearly understand their own styles so that they don't impose them on their children. They also need to identify their children's styles and adapt accordingly. Parents have a tendency to value their own abilities and then create expectations that their children will someday be able to do what they can do. For parents who are organized and thorough, it's frustrating when their kids are unstructured and don't do things properly. By recognizing their own styles, parents can understand where their expectations come from and then develop more accurate expectations of their kids based upon the children's styles, not their own.

Each child needs to be treated as an individual and yet, all too often, parents say, "I want to be fair to all of my kids, so I treat them all the same way." Actually, what is *fair* is to apply the Home Rule by treating each child the way he or she needs to be treated. To do this, parents must be able to read and react to the respective styles of their children.

When parents employ the *DISC* model, they may come to appreciate that their children are healthy and happy the way they are. Consider the following tendencies when identifying a child's style:

D children:

1. Crawl and walk early
2. Can be bossy with other children
3. React defiantly when they hear the word "No"
4. Insist upon their own rules, such as determining their own bedtime
5. Don't accept that others have authority over them, including teachers
6. Stubbornly demand what they want
7. Naturally lead others, controlling situations and people large and small
8. Throw temper tantrums when they lose or don't get their way
9. to win at everything, from games to the best toy to getting to stay up the latest
10. Are *always* on the move—doing, building, or rebuilding something

I children:

1. Happily get dirty or messy
2. Add comedy and practical jokes to everyday life
3. Have a limited attention span

4. Need constant stimulation
5. Have several groups of friends, such as neighborhood, school, and sports
6. Make up their own games or change the rules of existing games just to experience something new
7. Take big risks just to see what will happen (things don't always turn out well, but at least they get a good story to tell!)
8. Are happy to be the center of attention, whether it's in the classroom, at the dinner table, or on a stage
9. Can "sell ice to Eskimos" and can charm their way out of nearly anything
10. Easily exaggerate and apply selective use of facts to fit their needs

S children:
1. Take their time when learning to walk
2. Eat, drink, and move slowly and methodically
3. Go to bed without a fight
4. Get pleasure from helping others
5. Play by the rules of others
6. Bond strongly with a few close friends
7. Are slow to adapt to new activities and avoid taking risks
8. Let other children take the lead

9. Share their toys and play well with other children
10. Can be very shy and introverted

C children:

1. Don't like getting dirty, messy, or sticky
2. Have a gift for taking things apart to understand how they work and can then put them back together
3. Endlessly ask "why" and "what if" questions
4. Are comfortable with routines that create consistency and order in their schedule
5. Prefer mental challenges to physical games and can focus on one activity for long stretches
6. Get very upset when rules are broken
7. Have a smaller range of personal space than the other styles
8. Worry about and analyze things that might go wrong
9. Don't respond well to playful banter
10. Insist on a special place for everything

Parents who understand their own tendencies and accept their children's styles create the foundation for raising kids who are literally comfortable in their own skin. There's an old expression: *Don't try to teach a pig to sing. It will frustrate you and annoy the pig.* When we try to change others, we stifle their growth. When we accept others, we create an environment that cultivates their natural gifts and allows them to develop into the people they are meant to be. Shifting from judgment to understanding and acceptance helps foster self-esteem and creates well-adjusted children...*and adults.*

DISC Action Planning

Knowing is not enough, we must apply.
Willing is not enough, we must do.
—*Johann Wolfgang von Goethe*

There may be a number of people in your life with whom you can build better relationships by applying the *DISC* concepts. Select an individual, such as a friend, family member, or coworker, and answer the questions below:

What are my DISC strengths and how can I apply them with this person?

_____

_____

_____

Turn it down: What style do I need to exhibit less of to improve this relationship?

_____

_____

_____

Turn it up: What style do I need to exhibit more of to improve this relationship?

_____

_____

_____

Potential roadblocks: What are the obstacles that I am most likely to encounter?

_____

_____

_____

I will proactively overcome these barriers by…

_____

_____

_____

In addition to applying *DISC* to building better relationships, there may be situations or settings in which the styles can be more effectively applied. Select a *situation or setting* in which you can apply the *DISC* styles, and answer the following questions:

What are my DISC strengths and how can I apply them in this situation?

_____

_____

_____

Turn it down: What style do I need to exhibit less of to improve this situation?

_____

_____

_____

Turn it up: What style do I need to exhibit more of to improve this situation?

_____

_____

_____

Potential roadblocks: What are the obstacles that I am most likely to encounter?

_____

_____

_____

I will proactively overcome these barriers by...

_____

_____

_____

Onward

A chisel is just a tool to carve wood. But in the hands of a craftsman, it can create beautiful things. Likewise, the *DISC* is a tool for the mind. What can *you* build with it?

We have witnessed countless people develop deeper relationships, more rewarding careers, and more fulfilling lives. Tune into the styles of the people around you and set realistic expectations given their style. Recognize their intentions and treat people the way *they* want to be treated. Use your strengths, but avoid overusing them. And flexibly adapt your style to the people and situations you encounter. Unleash the power of *DISC* and your life will *Take Flight!*

Epilogue

Back at Home, dawn was breaking as our heroes gathered for breakfast at the dove family tree. Clark turned to Dorian and asked, "So, how has the eagle population taken to the behavioral styles?"

"I just focused on the bottom-line benefit and it didn't take long for them to see its value," said Dorian.

"Our clan was eager to explore every angle," said Crystal.

"They asked a lot questions," Clark added. "In fact, we have a few items to clarify with Xavier."

"If you can find him," said Indy with a grin.

"How about the doves?" Crystal asked Sarah.

"They were quiet for a while, so Samuel and I didn't know what to think. But later, we got great feedback that everyone took the styles to heart," Sarah said.

"Well, the parrots loved it!" Ivy volunteered. "We had a massive improv session and each of us acted out a style. I got to play Dorian. It was hilarious!"

"And where, exactly, did this take place? Not at the Council Tree, right?" taunted Dorian.

"Uhhh...ummm..." said Ivy.

"Moving right along," smiled Clark, "has anyone spoken to Xavier?"

"I heard Xavier was observing some humans camping next to his home," Samuel answered. "Evidently they were having some...*issues.*"

The birds all nodded knowingly.

Just a few feet from the group, a brownish-red figure slipped away unnoticed.

"Everyone has issues," thought Xavier, "but once people discover and embrace the styles, their worlds will change."

With a flick of his tail, he was gone, but there was still much work to be done....

The Authors

Merrick Rosenberg and Daniel Silvert have led training for more than 20,000 people in small and large corporations. They have worked with more than two-thirds of the current Fortune 100 companies in 44 states and around the world. Their clients include: AT&T, Bank of America, Blue Cross Blue Shield, Campbell Soup Company, Chase, Comcast, Ernst & Young, ExxonMobil, Ford Motor Company, Genentech, General Electric, Hewlett-Packard Company, Homeland Security, Johnson & Johnson, L3 Communications, L'Oreal, Nabisco, National Institute of Health, Novartis, Pepsi, PHH Mortgage, Pfizer, and the four main branches of the US armed forces.

The authors have been featured in the media as guests on shows such as, Money Matters Today on the Comcast Network and The Executive Leaders Radio Program. They have spoken for organizations, including: American Society of Training & Development, the Society for Human Resource Management, the Project Management Institute, the International Society for Performance Improvement, the Employer's Council, the American Society for Quality, Vistage International, the President's Club, and Young Associates.

Merrick Rosenberg, M.B.A., is an accomplished entrepreneur, speaker, and executive coach. In 1991, he co-founded Team Builders Plus, currently the largest and most recognized team building company in the United States. Merrick has led team and leadership development training programs to people around the world for more than two decades.

Drexel University honored Merrick as the Alumni Entrepreneur of the Year and NJ Biz selected him as a finalist for New Jersey Executive of the Year. Merrick was selected as one of the 40 People to Watch by SJ Magazine and has been profiled in the Philadelphia Business Journal.

Merrick's organization was recognized as the New Jersey Business of the Year, one of the Fastest Growing Companies in the U.S. by Inc. magazine, and as one of the Fastest Growing Companies in the Philadelphia region by the Philadelphia Business Journal.

Daniel Silvert, B.A., is an expert trainer and executive coach. As the VP of Learning & Development for Team Builders Plus, Dan designs and leads training programs at every level on teamwork, accountability, and transformational change. Dan has brought his unique perspective to hundreds of companies, non-profits, and government agencies including W.L. Gore, L'Oreal, L-3 Communications, Merck, Blue Cross Blue Shield, Dow Jones, Home Depot, and the Department of Homeland Security.